Linda,
It's b
with
need to get together when
we've reached our
Optimal Level !!
Liz

Optimal Level:

A Woman's Guide to
Meeting Life's Challenges

Printed in Victoria, Canada

Note for Librarians: a cataloguing record for this book that includes Dewey Classification and US Library of Congress numbers is available from the National Library of Canada. The complete cataloguing record can be obtained from the National Library's online database at: www.nlc-bnc.ca/amicus/index-e.html
ISBN 1-4120-2174-X

TRAFFORD

This book was published on-demand in cooperation with Trafford Publishing. On-demand publishing is a unique process and service of making a book available for retail sale to the public taking advantage of on-demand manufacturing and Internet marketing. On-demand publishing includes promotions, retail sales, manufacturing, order fulfilment, accounting and collecting royalties on behalf of the author.

Suite 6E, 2333 Government St., Victoria, B.C. V8T 4P4, CANADA

Phone	250-383-6864	Toll-free	1-888-232-4444 (Canada & US)
Fax	250-383-6804	E-mail	sales@trafford.com
Web site	www.trafford.com	TRAFFORD PUBLISHING IS A DIVISION OF TRAFFORD
HOLDINGS LTD.			

Trafford Catalogue #03-2723   www.trafford.com/robots/03-2723.html

10   9   8   7   6   5   4   3   2

Table of Contents

Acknowledgments

Special thanks and great appreciation to my husband, Mike, for his love, unending support, and mutual workaholic tendencies. To my daughter, Laura, who is always there for me, from the constant daily tasks to my neediest times when her support, love, resourcefulness, and creativity continue to astound me. Without her, I probably would not have been able to find the time to finish this book. Thanks also to my son, Brad, from whom I continue to learn important social/business skills, and to my mom, from whom I learned to persevere. To my father and aunt Lyl, both deceased. Without them I would not have known what is possible. Loving thanks also to my cousins Shari Kravitz and Carole Davis, and to my steadfast friend Judi Edenson for their endearing love, and the chance to develop my budding facilitating skills for Feminine Forum. To Linda Brakeall, Irene Rozansky and Candy Wertheimer for their love, support, and inspiration. Big thanks to our editor, Diane Valletta, who really pulled this project together for us. –**Linda**

As I mentioned in this book, my husband, Chuck, has been my anchor as I have done multiple projects. This time was no exception. I thank him for his support and inspiration in encouraging me to grow and develop. My girls, Lisa, Stacy and Tanya, have been my shining stars. I thank Linda for sticking with me and allowing Stacy to do the graphic design and layout for this book.

Thanks also to Barbara Newsom for her help with editing the book content for accuracy in applying the DiSC® concepts. Barb, Diane Wilson, Lorraine Cardwell, Anna Weselak and Teresa Nieves have been an inspiration for me, having successfully started their consulting businesses years ago and given me valuable lessons in business success.

In the last months I have been working with the Behavioral Health Unit at San Juan Regional Medical Center in Farmington, NM. I thank the staff for their support and excitement as I have plodded to get this book to the publisher. –**Liz**

About The Authors

Linda McCabe has set and reached many goals in her life. A graduate of the University of Illinois at Champaign-Urbana, Linda began her career in publishing, but eventually turned to teaching in Chicago Public Schools. After 15 years of teaching, she made a bold move to join her father's business, H. Diamond Iron & Metal Co. Linda worked her way up, became President, and grew the business to $6 million in sales.

Following a dream, she sold H. Diamond and launched Feminine Forum (www.feminineforum.com). From piles of scrap metal, she feels she has learned a heap of lessons which have helped her dedicate herself to helping women discover their real life values, meet their goals, and follow their hearts.

Feminine Forum is made up of groups of women who meet once a month at various locations. Through these discussions women learn, share and grow. The main purpose of these meetings is to promote the empowerment of women toward achieving their goals.

Linda lives in a Northwest suburb of Illinois, has been married for 33 years to a husband she describes as a good candidate for One of The World's Best Husbands, and has two wonderful adult children who she adores.

Apart from family, friends, work, and country, Linda also loves weight lifting, running, reading, and movies. In addition, she has a passionate interest in supporting and guiding women, and in working with them to reach solutions, to explore new, exciting directions, and to propel them toward vigorously successful results.

Liz Peterson attended Fairview Hospital School of Nursing in Minneapolis and received her license as a Registered Nurse. Twenty years later she completed her B.S. in Allied Health/Psychology from the University of South Dakota at Vermillion, South Dakota. Ten years later she received her executive MBA from North Park University in Chicago. She is a proponent of the life-long learning process.

After years of working in the healthcare field, Liz incorporated Business Training & Consulting (www.train4success.com) in 1999. With an independent spirit and love for a challenge, she followed her dream of becoming an entrepreneur and doing what she loved. She currently works with executives, managers, and their staff either in organizations or coaching independently. Liz uses Inscape Publishing's Personal Profile System®, an instrument widely used in corporate training and coaching, to help individuals maximize their strengths by assessing their preferred behavioral style.

Consulting, training and coaching on issues related to leadership/team development are Liz's strengths. Her passion is to create a work environment where people love to work, and can use their creative and intellectual talents. She believes that successful companies in the 21st century will value the knowledge, skills and abilities each person has to offer.

Like Linda, Liz has proven that you can have both career and family. She has been married for over 30 years to the same man! As one of her friends has said, "he is the anchor, the stabilizing force." And as she flies off to the next endeavor, no one has been more supportive. Liz has three daughters, all having inherited an independent, free spirit. She is very fortunate to have all of them living in the Chicagoland area where she resides.

Introduction

The purpose of this book is to help you function at an Optimal Level, in order to gain more control over how you respond to life's challenges.

We are all born with unique personalities, which we cannot change. However, we can change our behaviors; we can choose how we respond to who we are, where we are, and what we are.

In this book we want to focus on what we do have control over – our behaviors. The book's structure is based on the four unique behavioral styles defined by the DiSC® behavioral assessment model from Inscape Publishing, Inc. The four quadrant behavior styles in this model are dominant, influencing, steadiness and conscientiousness. Throughout this book, these behavior styles will be represented by four characters named Hillary, Ivana, Laura and Martha.

First you'll complete an assessment to discover your preferred style. Then we'll explore together how each of the styles approach and respond to life issues, and the choices we have for how to maximize our strengths and deal with our weaknesses.

By no means are we trying to put you into a box. We do know from years of experience, however, that most women are more comfortable operating out of one or two modes of behavior. Regardless of your style preferences, we think you'll gain insights on how to deal with your challenges in the most effective manner.

We are laying the groundwork to help you see the importance of being aware of who you are and what may be best for you. If you are at a point where your self-esteem is suffering, your anxiety is increasing, your energy level draining, the monster under the bed is rearing its ugly head, or you just feel confused or discouraged, we invite you to read on.

Guiding Principles

In conceiving and in writing this book, there are a few principles that both guided and mean a lot to the authors. We want to share them with you.

To put forth the best use of our knowledge and backgrounds. Information in this book is based on our past knowledge and current research. As authors, we have come from entirely different backgrounds. Yet this book is presented in a format that will open women's eyes to some of the behaviors that may be causing them problems, and one to which we hope every woman can relate.

Liz has worked extensively with the DiSC® model from Inscape Publishing, Inc. in her coaching, training and consulting business. Linda has worked extensively with women. Listening to women's challenges, concerns and frustrations is part of her role in leading her Feminine Forum groups, where she facilitates meetings on best methods to respond and actions to take.

To offer choices. It is our intention to offer suggestions only rather than advice. We want to offer possibilities as opposed to telling you what to do. It is up to you, the reader, to apply the knowledge to your daily living if it is desirable and applicable.

To offer opportunity to be more aware. Each of us has our own perception of how things are and what we need to do to make things better for ourselves. The problem usually occurs when we don't do what we know will improve our situations or we have a blind spot regarding our problems. If our problem is not being aware of how and what is affecting us adversely, we could ask a friend or coach to help us see our blind spots.

Perhaps during a seminar on self-awareness you participated in an exercise called the Johari Window. This is an awareness concept named after Joseph Luft and Harry Ingham. It was first used in an information session at the Western Training Laboratory in Group Development in 1955.

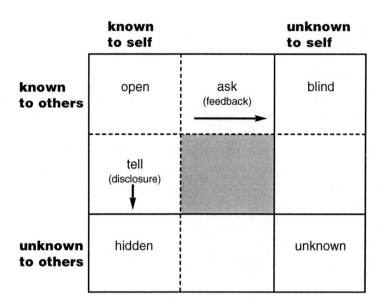

What the four panes of the Johari Window signify:

Open: The open area represents our conscious self: our attitudes, behavior, motivation, values, or our way of life. We are aware of ourselves in this area. We freely disclose ourselves to others in this area. We are an "open book."

Hidden: Others cannot know our hidden area unless we disclose it. In this area we consciously keep things within ourselves and often retain, out of fear, our secrets. The degree to which we share ourselves with others (disclosure) is the degree to which we can be known.

Blind: There are things about ourselves that we do not know but that others can see more clearly; or things we believe to be true of ourselves for a variety of reasons but others do not see at all. When others say what they see (feedback) in a supportive, responsible way, we are able to hear it and use this feedback to become more enlightened about ourselves. We can then test the reality of who we are and choose to change what is affecting us.

Unknown: We are more complex and have many more assets than that

which we know now. From time to time something happens; we may begin to feel, read, hear or dream something that is revealed to us from our unconscious mind. Then we "know" what we have never "known" before.

It is through disclosure and feedback that our Open pane is expanded and we gain access to the potential within us, represented by the Unknown pane. In this book we are attempting to help you discover and know what you may never have known before.

We'd also like to help you reduce your Blind pane. This pane has frequently been referred to as our "Blind Spot." This pane can affect another person's view of us without our knowing what is going on. We wonder, "Why did they respond to us in that way?" It also affects our knowing what it is about ourselves that would be good to change, had we been aware. The larger our Open pane, the more we can grow and develop.

To employ excellent standards. We have applied our highest ethical standards to writing this book. We have carefully researched our material, and feel we have dispensed our information in a format designed to reveal behaviors that may be causing women's greatest challenges.

To be beneficial to women. We seek to use our knowledge, skill, and abilities to provide clarity and purpose to all who strive to grow and develop into more satisfied and healthy people. We believe whatever we print in this book will be of benefit to women who choose to use some of the suggestions that apply to their situation and behavioral style.

To continue a tradition for empowerment. Two women trailblazers who lived in the 1800's, Susan B. Anthony and Elizabeth Cady Stanton, believed in a program of social, economic, and political reform. They sought to change not only the legal status of women but also the way society viewed the very role of women. Before and since their times, women have had to overcome gender socialization patterns. It is our binding principle that by combining recognition of a woman's unique personality characteristics with general solutions for issues women face daily, we can contribute to empowerment for all women in every aspect of their lives.

Behavioral Styles and Assessment

As women, we sometimes feel we have very little control over anything. At times we can feel so helpless, so vulnerable, so abused… so stressed, frustrated, angry or tired.

Behaviors are an important part of how we deal with challenges, concerns and frustrations. Sometimes our behaviors and attitudes can cause us problems. We may get so comfortable in a victim's role or the blaming role that it gives us an excuse to avoid taking responsibility for anything. Or we may think or feel that we were born into the wrong family, had parents who constantly told us how bad or worthless we were, had siblings who teased us and constantly picked on us, went to the wrong school, or lived in the wrong part of the city. These feelings and beliefs can cause us to act in ways that are detrimental to us.

How is it that someone else can grow up in the same family, live in the same part of the city, have some of the same physical characteristics, and view life entirely differently? We can say we are a product of our heredity, our environment or anything else. The more excuses we can find, the more we can feel justified in remaining stuck and blaming someone else for our plight.

One thing we DO have control over is our behaviors – how we think, feel and act. For example, if we think life has treated us badly, we will feel like a victim and act helpless. We will display behaviors of helplessness. On the other hand, if we think that, no matter how life has treated us, we are responsible for how we think, feel and act, then we will accept the things we cannot change and change the things we can. This is not always easy. Sometimes it takes the help of others, but it can be done.

We do not have a choice in changing personality. Each of us has a personality that is more introverted or extroverted, is more sensing or intuitive, is more feeling or thinking, and is more judging or perceptive. Each personality is valuable and helps maintain balance in our relationships, our homes, our jobs and our environment. You may have completed a Myers-Briggs Type Inventory and have insight into your own personality traits. You can read more about personality types in the book, Do What You Are, by Paul D. Tieger and Barbara Barron-Tieger.

When we are operating in our most comfortable style, we have more confidence and more energy, and are usually happier people. To operate at this optimal level, we need to be aware of what our most comfortable style is. Some of us have more "flex" among the behaviors than others do; we may easily adapt to another style.

If we enjoy being by ourselves, we usually do not become budding socialites but may choose to become excellent philosophers or writers. Why is it that writers have such a hard time promoting their books? Most are highly successful because they work best by processing internally. It is uncomfortable to be out socializing. Would a marketing person make a good computer programmer? Perhaps, depending on determination and fortitude. But they may be constantly drained of energy and very unhappy. You can see the problems caused when a parent who has an entirely different style than her child insists that the child enter the same occupation that the parent has loved and thrived on. It often doesn't work!

When you are aware of which style suits you best, you can choose ways that are most comfortable to deal with insecurities and stressors. Some of these insecurities and stressors may be handled best by changing the way we think about them. Others may be handled by more active measures.

Finding Your Behavioral Style

To get started let's take a brief assessment of how you best respond to situations in your everyday life. This is not a test. It's a tool to help you identify your strengths.

First, complete the Behavioral Style Assessment to determine your preferred style. Many people have a combination of preferred styles. However, when analyzing your behavior, you can determine, within a certain margin of accuracy, a tendency toward one of the categories. There are no right or wrong answers and there are no best or worst ways to behave. So just observe yourself, take it very lightly, and answer the questions below as best you can. This assessment will serve quite well, giving you some guidelines on the one or two types that are most closely related to your preferred style.

Behavioral Styles Assessment

Circle only the "yes" in the statements that are true for you most of the time. If there are two "yes" columns, circle both of them. At the end add up the "yes" responses under each of the names. Whichever name has the most "yes" responses is probably your preferred style. If you have two names with a similar number of responses, it is likely that you have two preferred behavioral styles. This is not uncommon.

	Hillary	Ivana	Laura	Martha
1. Would you prefer to work with people?	No	Yes	Yes	No
2. Do you initiate conversation with people that you do not know?	No	Yes	No	No
3. Are you quiet and reserved?	No	No	Yes	Yes
4. Do you approach people indirectly?	No	No	Yes	Yes
5. Are you extremely competitive?	Yes	No	No	No
6. Do you value accuracy?	No	No	No	Yes
7. Do you often tell people what to do?	Yes	No	No	No
8. Do you usually ask people what they want to do?	No	No	Yes	No
9. Are you usually content to leave things unchanged?	No	No	Yes	No
10. Do you like a fast paced environment?	Yes	Yes	No	No
11. Do you prefer a slower pace?	No	No	Yes	Yes
12. Do you frequently speak in a loud voice?	Yes	Yes	No	No

	Hillary	Ivana	Laura	Martha
13. Is your speech quiet and subdued?	No	No	Yes	Yes
14. Are you usually impatient?	Yes	No	No	No
15. Is getting cooperation from others important to you?	No	No	Yes	No
16. Do you prefer to withhold your feelings from others?	Yes	No	No	Yes
17. Are you very expressive with your feelings?	No	Yes	No	No
18. Do you prefer to be traditional and keep things the way they are currently?	No	No	Yes	No
19. Do you tend to show little emotion?	Yes	No	No	Yes
20. Do you usually want to know "what"?	Yes	No	No	No
21. Do you usually want to know "who"?	No	Yes	No	No
22. Do you usually want to know "how"?	No	No	Yes	No
23. Do you usually want to know "why"?	No	No	No	Yes
24. Are you very sure of yourself?	Yes	No	No	No
25. Is your preference based on quality and analysis?	No	No	No	Yes
26. Is your home or office especially well organized?	No	No	No	Yes

27. Do you always want to win?	Yes	No	No	No
28. Do you weigh all the facts before making a decision?	No	No	No	Yes
29. Are you impulsive at times?	No	Yes	No	No
30. Are you frequently forceful in your actions?	Yes	No	No	No
31. Are you usually calm and friendly?	No	No	Yes	No
32. Do you go ahead with projects before the team has agreed on actions?	Yes	No	No	No
33. Are you the life of the party?	No	Yes	No	No
34. Are you easy-going?	No	No	Yes	No
35. Do you usually seek challenges?	Yes	No	No	No
36. Do you hate to be the center of attention?	No	No	Yes	No
37. Is your schedule usually overbooked?	No	Yes	No	No
38. Are you extremely confident?	Yes	No	No	No
39. Would you prefer to work on a team and in a group?	No	No	Yes	No
40. Do you see things positively?	No	Yes	No	No
41. Do you refuse to give in?	Yes	No	No	No
42. Are you very analytical?	No	No	No	Yes

	Hillary	Ivana	Laura	Martha
43. Do you feel relaxed most of the time?	No	Yes	No	No
44. Are you the first to act on something?	Yes	No	No	No
45. Are you detail oriented?	No	No	No	Yes
46. Do you find it easy to meet strangers?	No	Yes	No	No
47. Do others see you as powerful?	Yes	No	No	No
48. Do you usually seek other people's approval?	No	Yes	Yes	No
49. Do you need all of the evidence before making decisions?	No	No	No	Yes
50. Are you a very talkative person?	No	Yes	No	No
51. Do you usually want to make the rules?	Yes	No	No	No
Yes Totals:	_____	_____	_____	_____

Add up your scores by counting the number of yes entries in each column.

Which column has the most Yes entries? _____
You are most like this character.

Now that you have a better idea of which character is most like you, take this information and focus on that character in the next sections of this book. (For example, if your score for the character "Hilary" is the highest, pay most attention to how Hilary can make changes to improve how she thinks, feels and acts. The same applies to the other characters.)

As mentioned above, we have chosen four distinctive names of people to describe each behavioral style:

- **Hillary** functions best in the dominant role. She likes to have control, be the boss, and tell others what to do.

- **Ivana** prefers to function in a very outgoing, lively style. She enjoys having the spotlight and loves to get recognition for what she does.

- **Laura** prefers to be in family oriented environments and is more quiet and friendly. She enjoys life when everyone is cooperating and people appreciate her support.

- **Martha** values accuracy and pays attention to detail. She likes it when all the t's are crossed, the i's are dotted and everything is in its place.

None of these people are better than the other. We need each for balance. One may certainly irritate the other because of various behaviors, but when each understands the importance of having the other styles, it is easier to accept the other person for what she is.

Problems usually occur when one person does not understand and respect the other's strengths and weaknesses, or when one's strengths become too overpowering or weaknesses highlighted. It can happen with any one behavioral style. Hillary can become domineering. Ivana can become attention seeking. Laura can isolate from the pressure. Martha can try to make everything too perfect. When anyone becomes too much of one particular style, it becomes a problem for others and for the person herself.

How To Use This Book

After completing the assessment, there are two approaches to take in reading or working with the rest of this book.

1. If there is a burning issue, say, life balance, that you feel needs to have your immediate attention, then go to that chapter first. Though we've all had to deal with every issue in this book, one or two may seem to have had an overwhelming impact for you at some time in your life.

2. On the other hand, if you have about the same level of interest in all the issues, then start with the first chapter.

The book is set up in a workbook style. We suggest you purchase a new, attractive notebook or diary-stylebook with blank pages to use as a journal. Or use the Notepad at the back of this book. You are welcome to use the pages in this book to record your exercise results. However, you may have thoughts and questions you'll want to jot down in your journal – or you may want to get more creative, requiring more room than these pages allow.

Always read the introduction to the chapter to get a good overview of that issue. Following the overview, sets of solutions organized according to behavioral style are presented. After reading the introduction, go first to the character representing the behavioral style that dominated your assessment. Then read the solutions, one at a time. There's usually an exercise recommended for each solution. Depending on how you feel most comfortable, you can either scan through the entire set of solutions for your behavioral type, or stop after each one.

In either case – whether you scan through or read and stop after one solution, do the exercises in the order they are listed.

The solutions and exercises are arranged with purpose, in a calculated order, to take you from one point of awareness and recognition to a broader and broader appreciation of causes, beliefs, and revelations. We believe the order and the following processes will aid you in becoming more familiar with your own characteristics and behavior. As a result, you'll gain the power to alter that behavior to serve you better.

Now onward to fun exercises, happy discoveries, and dazzling behavioral differences!

~one~
Self-Image

"You're a bad girl."

"You look awful in that!"

"If you act that way, what boy is going to like you?"

Perhaps you didn't hear those particular comments from your mom or dad when you were little. However, you could certainly recall similar remarks you did hear from your parents or other authority figures. Those kinds of comments bring to mind the rings around a tree. They mark a groove into our psyches and leave a definite impression. Those verbal descriptions, along with how our parents held us as infants and reacted to us, are the beginning of how we construct our picture of ourselves.

It is true that we also receive positive comments as well when our parents deemed our behavior as deserving praise. Of course, the momentary picture of the way we see ourselves changes depending on the frequency and intensity of these kinds of messages, as well as who is saying them. We also hear judgments about ourselves proclaimed by relatives, teachers, friends, employers, doctors, clergymen, and others who have influence on us as we grow and trek through our lives. We internalize our experiences and our perception of new situations are colored by those earlier messages.

That picture – our self-image – may be definitely etched with a disadvantage simply because we were born girls. True, things have improved to some degree. The point, however, is that girls frequently are more likely to develop a negative picture because of our culture. It wasn't too long ago when we had very few role models. In a large part it was strictly the male power figures in our culture and society who became successful and famous. Maybe our brothers were told they could do things that we could not; whether that was climbing trees, throwing a ball further, or going for their career choices that made more sense for a boy than a girl.

As females we may have learned we weren't strong, and needed men to do things for us or that we had to be good, quiet, and ladylike. Many fathers may have been disappointed that they didn't have a male offspring. As females, being aggressive was a quality to be avoided. We were told to be good at taking care of our men. The fact that we had to dress a certain way to be fashionable limited our sense of individuality, creating a lack of identity to a certain extent. The boyfriend we chose or who chose us further defined us.

So take a look back. Who and what influenced you to become what you see when you ask yourself, "Who am I?"

Even when we have strong successes, isn't it true that, at times, an annoying voice whispers to you that somehow you are a fraud. You know that voice that makes some comment that creates a feeling of embarrassment because you know that you are a fake compared to others in your field who have reached your level of accomplishment. We are so hard on ourselves, and it's mostly because of the conditioning we received simply because we were born girls.

Let's see how the negative messages we may have received, may have impacted us. Some of us may repeat these messages to ourselves in negative self-talk. Let's see if you recognize some of the highlights of your self-image:

• Do you feel drained? No matter how you pump yourself up, do you wind up completely devoid of energy?

• Do you think you are not good enough, pretty enough, talented enough, smart enough, sexy enough, clever enough, schooled enough, tough enough – for whatever you would like to have, do, or be?

• Do you give up your power by buying into what you perceive to be the messages you get from your husband, significant other, children, parents, co-workers, friends, or relatives? Do you allow their opinions, or what you perceive to be their opinions, define who you are? Do you give your personal power to others by allowing what they say or you think they mean by viewing yourself according to their beliefs about you?

• Do you consistently set your standards so high, or keep raising the bar, so that whatever you do or accomplish gets devalued and you never achieve your goals? That way you can always see yourself as being less than what is okay or good.

• Do you set up fears that keep you from reaching your goals?

• Are you too fat, thin, short, tall, pretty, ugly or dress wrong?

• Are you often physically ill?

• Are you often emotionally disturbed?

• Do you keep yourself so busy that you never have an opportunity to feel okay about yourself?

If you answered yes to more than one of these questions, you may have some serious self-image work for yourself!

Well, that's actually positive. You've reached the stage beyond self-enforced delusion or semi-unconsciousness. You have admitted to the need for self-image surgery. Take a moment and congratulate yourself. That's right. You are familiar with the well-known fact that baby steps lead to learning how to walk. You have taken a first major step. The next thing you must learn – right now – is to acknowledge when you have taken a step toward improving or growing. Do not underestimate the importance of this accomplishment.

Realizing that something you're doing – whether in thought alone or behavior – is keeping you from going in the direction you desire, is necessary before you can even begin your journey toward whatever success you seek. Even if that success is only to discover what you do to retard your growth. So, go some place private and shout. Shout, "Yeah! I just took one great big baby step toward where I want to be!"

With your behavioral style in mind, let's get on with that next little step. We will take a look at the belief system you start with, and do some more self-assessment. Then we'll follow some mini-steps to creating harmony with your thoughts and actions in order to successfully create the results you'd like to have in your life.

Solutions for self-image:

Hillary

Solution # 1: Take time for self

Schedule time for yourself by using your calendar to block out definite only-for-you time. Find time to read (not industry or books related to work) or do crossword puzzles, or whatever you do that you enjoy. Become aware of what to do that reduces stress, and focus on something you can do that will not create pressure for you to accomplish a goal. That may be gardening, reading a book and having a decaf coffee treat at a local bookstore, a candlelit bath, a bicycle ride, a movie with a friend, or anything that doesn't feel like pressure to be good or perform in any way. Find something that you want to do, for the sheer enjoyment of doing it and also to experience pleasure.

Solution # 2: Get off autopilot

Keeping yourself on an "activity treadmill" blocks out your self-awareness. You operate on automatic, and you lose the perfect you that's covered up inside. Look for what you do in your life that allows you to hide from your emotions and from your feelings, such as staying too long at work or over exercising, piling on to do's and activities so you don't have any quiet time just to think or enjoy life. You may be afraid of what you'll find and that could create stress. The sooner you look at what's going on inside, the sooner you can start to heal and become a whole person.

Solution #3: Gain inner harmony

Find some way to get back in touch with your spirit. Find time to meditate. Maybe take a bath, get a massage. Listen to tapes, take a nature walk, garden, or journal. These are not escape mechanisms; do not choose reading, movies, and other vehicles in order to escape to another world. The key here is to look at getting in touch with you inner being. Sit alone quietly by yourself for five or 10 minutes each day to let yourself become aware of you, of what is real, and of what you truly want.

Solution #4: Get physical exercise

Stretching, pilates, or yoga. You need those endorphins. So be sure to schedule regular sessions for exercise in order to develop and restore your physical being.

Solution #5: Define your own success

Do you really need to be accomplishing results at all times? Don't give up your power by striving for someone else's goals of success. Take a couple of hours to examine your internal values to determine what success means for you: Money? A beautiful home? Happy children? A fulfilling career? Contributing to your world?

Solution #6: Relax and enjoy the process of achieving the results you want

We actually get resistance when we push too hard to get results. Do "what if?" exercises. Ask yourself, "What if I didn't reach this goal, what would be the worse thing that would happen?" Are you going to die? Will your life be over? You have to learn to relax, and let go sometimes to get where you want to be.

Solution #7: Get plenty of rest

Determine what your body needs as far as number of hours of sleep. Select a night when you do not set the alarm. And see how many hours you slept. Do that again the next month. After awhile you will be able to determine how many hours of sleep you body naturally requires.

Solution #8: Decrease stress

Do things like counting to 10 before blowing your cork. When you're angry, take five minutes out of your day to be quiet, give yourself a neck massage, lie out in the sun if you can, listen to some soft music, etc. If you do things that relieve your stress, you will feel like less of a tyrant. You will begin to feel that people actually like you better and will serve as bet-

ter cohorts for you in attaining your goals.

Ivana

Solution #1: Become aware of your value

You may be keeping score by how much attention you are getting. Do self-assessment exercises. Make a list of all of your positive traits. Become aware of your need to be the center of attention. Practice being alone sometimes, and see if you can feel okay with that experience. When you do this, you will better be able to gain awareness of who you are. Also, ask others what they like about you. Begin to focus on your own belief system.

Solution #2: Do a brief retrospective

Examine the messages you received from parents, teachers, and authority figures. Try to remember what behavior elicited praise and goodies. Notice your behavior now, as an adult, and see if your behavior demonstrates that you're still operating based on those past messages. Go to the note pages at the end of this book and write down some of the interactions you're having with others. Analyze them to see if you are getting the results you want. Can you think of ways to behave differently with your evolved, adult expectations of yourself?

Solution #3: Banish the "shoulds"

This exercise is similar to doing a brief retrospective, but a shade different. Ask yourself: "Am I able to feel OK with myself even when I don't have enough energy to be the center of attention?" Write a list of everything that represents your picture of what you expect yourself to be when you are around other people. Be honest about this. Once you have your list, you can edit out what you think you are doing just to please others, or to get people to like you. Come from your own values and decide how you really want to be, based on your own standards and values, and not the "Shoulds" you felt previously compelled to follow.

Solution #4: Seek inner harmony

Attend religious services with other people. Join spirituality classes. Find and go on group retreats.

Solution #5: Find ways to gain mastery of your emotions

Start to notice how you see yourself coming across to others. Note how flamboyant you are when something is not going your way. You don't want to turn people off, don't you agree? When you are worked up about some issue, count to 10 before you speak Go to the note pages in the back of this book, and spend about one hour writing down three times when your actions or comments have hurt, angered or embarrassed someone. Rewrite those scenarios and describe what you would like to do instead in the future when similar circumstances occur. Pretend you are an actress in a movie and redo the scene to make it more socially appropriate.

Laura

Solution #1: Believe in self and self-acceptance

List your strengths and positive traits. Even if you think you may not have a certain trait now, ask yourself if one time in your life you did. Think about a time in your past when you felt so good about a particular behavior, a time when you were so proud of yourself, a time when you glowed knowing you liked some way you were. Accept that quality as part of you that you don't see that often. If it was there once, it is most likely still a part of you.

You are loyal and make other people feel good about themselves. You are supportive of others' goals and accomplishments. You do the grunt work, and allow others to take credit. Choose a trait that you like but believe you do not often display. Work on redeveloping that characteristic. As an example, you may not be the person leading a project; however, you are a very good second in command. If you look back, you will see that in school, or within an organization, or on the job, you did this role very well. First, take credit for it. Stay conscious about strengthening this behavior, and you will see that you can actually re-create that latent trait and accept that new positive part of you. Then choose another positive quality you know you had at one time and work on that, and so on.

Solution #2: Take time for yourself

Work on fun things that feel good, such as reading, seeing funny movies, and finding things that make you laugh. Take a bubble bath, get a massage, take a bicycle or canoe ride, take a child to an amusement park, swing on a swing in the park, etc.

Solution #3: Assess yourself

Search magazines for pictures that you can use to make a collage to support you in recognizing yourself and acknowledging your accomplishments. Create a list of special treats you'd like someone to do for or with you. Then decide on which friend or relative you'll ask to do that treat for or with you.

Solution #4: Learn to master your emotions

There are several ways to develop control over your emotions. One method that can help you learn to express your emotions is to talk with someone you trust in a one-on-one setting. Choose an appropriate place and time, think in advance about what you want to express, and slowly work up to telling that someone how you feel. Another technique that will help you master your emotions is to keep a journal or find a creative outlet such as drawing. Spend quiet time writing about your thoughts or expressing them by drawing.

Another, perhaps more comfortable, method to draw feelings out, is to approach this as a game player. If you have many fears and worries, write them down. For each one you have written, go back and think of the worst outcome that could happen. Write those scenarios down. Then begin to exaggerate those pictures more. Start to make them silly to the point where you can laugh about them. By exaggerating these fears and worries, you can start to see how ridiculous they may be, and how they are more your creation than reality.

Solution #5: Increase physical well-being

Walk with a friend daily, start bicycling, or join a nearby health club.

Solution #6: Examine your negative self-talk

Take steps to stop your negative self-talk by listening to what you say to yourself. Acknowledge that you can rephrase the comments you make to yourself. When you hear the negative chatter, gently remind yourself that you can stop, and replace your remark with a more positive slant. Ask yourself what you truly believe about what you said. Then decide if there is some action you'd like to take so that you do not form that opinion about yourself, and can avoid having to say the same thing to yourself in the future. Continue this habit. There are some tools you may want to use to reinforce this rephrasing practice.

• Consider putting a ribbon, special color ring, or rubber band around your finger or wrist.

• Pretend you have a tape recorder in your head. When you catch your self saying something negative about yourself, press the imaginary button and make some silly silent sound in your head to represent the sound that is made when rewinding the tape. Or use a buzzer sound similar to one on a game show when the wrong answer is given.

• Carry a small notebook with you and use positive reinforcement Every time you successfully change a negative thought into a positive one, put a mark down in your notebook. At the end of a week, count your marks. Develop a number system. As an example, for five marks, you get a special cup of coffee you like. For 10 points, you get a half hour stroll through a bookstore. For more points, give yourself some other special treat in which you rarely indulge.

Martha

Solution #1: Belief in self and self-acceptance

At times you may be very hard on yourself. Take a look back at how you developed your belief system. What messages have you accepted from your childhood? Try to challenge those beliefs. For instance, were you told that to be a good girl, you needed to be neat, or soft-spoken, or realized that girls were supposed to be pretty? Write down what you believe women are supposed to be. Write down what you genuinely feel you want to be. Ask yourself if there are times when you feel the need to be perfect. Start experimenting to see if you could lower your standards just a little at first, and see how you feel. If that works, try another belief concept, and see how you can adjust that to how you want to be now. For instance, following are some belief concepts you may want to challenge:

- Need to be unselfish and nice

- Need to be a lady

- Need to be thin and beautiful

- Need to be super responsible and trustworthy

- Need to be everything to everybody.

Solution #2: Banish the "shoulds"

Examine your expectations to see if they are based in reality. You probably deserve a break. One way to do this is to stop before a decision about some daily activity, and ask yourself what would happen if you did this differently – or not at all? Or simply delay your activity and do something completely unplanned or directly opposite of what you would normally do. Instead, do something relaxing, something unregimented, something seemingly for no purpose. That something could be watching TV, browsing in a hardware store, looking at goldfish in a pet store, etc.

Solution #3: Get physical exercise

Since you normally are pretty regimented and stick to your routines, plan one exercise appointment to do something different. If you normally do yoga, try hiking instead. If you normally do aerobics or step, play tennis instead with a friend (even if you stink at it!) Or even better, just this once, do not exercise. Use the spirit of abandon to loosen up by doing something different, and see how you feel; see whether the world comes to an end.

Solution #4: Decrease stress

Write a list of things that you feel have you stressed out. Even though it may be difficult, prioritize your list. Choose the top two circumstances that are causing you the most stress. Now become a playwright. Create scenes and write them down. First, describe what would happen if suddenly you were paralyzed or even disappeared. How would the situation change? Secondly, write a scene describing yourself as totally irresponsible, lazy, nice but caring much less. What would happen now? You will probably start to feel less intense and come to see that problems can be dealt with or solved with less narrowness and intensity, and that you can lighten up a bit and still resolve or handle the situation. Later you can do the same thing with other matters causing you stress.

Solution #5: Return to the child

To gain more energy and to alleviate the feeling of being drained often, again you will serve yourself well to adopt abandon. That is, turn your efforts to giving yourself permission to be okay as you are without having to be correct, or meeting your own set of high standards. Do something such as paint an abstract picture – no boundaries to stay in, no form, and no structure. Splatter, let colors run, pick the wrong colors that do not match! Use food, flowers, and anything with texture. Only tear up the flowers, let the grains be too thick in one place and too thin in the other. Fly in the face of what you think looks good or right. Breathe deeply when doing this and ask yourself to smile as much as possible. Hang up your masterpiece on your bathroom mirror. Remind yourself that the process of creation is freeing – without restrictions and set rules. You can accomplish the same results by playing a child's game, playing in a child's playground on slides and seesaws, or watching a child's TV show and playing along with a child.

Solution #6: Renew friendships and seek new ones

Think carefully about your good, solid friends. Decide with whom you would want to spend some time. Think carefully about your core values. Then examine your friendships based on who truly likes and loves you, who supports you, who fills a need in you to be good or giving, and not based on who meets your high standards of behavior or is necessarily "easier" to control. Consider joining women's groups or taking advanced classes in courses to which you are drawn to meet women who have similar interests. Go slowly to reveal yourself as you get to know your new friends. However, come from a basic trust. Tread slowly, but allow yourself to be open to finding new friends who truly care about you and will support and nurture you.

~two~
Life Balance

Do it all!

Be beautiful, youthful, intelligent, successful, a cook, a woman who runs or does pilates for exercise… be a reader of fiction and non-fiction… be a mother, a chauffeur… be understanding, sexy, stylish, a great gardener, a skilled traveler, a wonderful friend, a fully educated and knowledgeable person, funny, unselfish, skilled at the computer…shall we go on? This list could be as long as this page, and still wouldn't be an exaggeration.

Watching a video of a working mother, a female business owner, or even a compulsive, single workaholic on any given day would make the viewer exhausted. Women are amazing!

Working with women has revealed to us that at the top of their list of critical issues is finding balance in life.

First let's consider the meaning of balance. One meaning is "equality between the totals of the two sides of an account." Another is "an aesthetically pleasing integration of elements." Life balance for women is about the second definition. According to physical law, perfect balance never exists without producing a loss to one side or the other because of all things being in a constant state of change. Keep in mind that balancing one's own life is a personal matter. It is what is "aesthetically pleasing" to you. We do not want to remain static. We want instead to bring about an environment and behavior that fosters stability and maintains a state of operational comfort.

The dilemma of balancing work, family, errands and chores, social and spiritual life, recreation and personal pursuits comes from much the same influence discussed in Chapter I on self-image – namely, the messages and tapes to which we listen. Stop and look at the cause behind our madness to do it all and be everything to everyone. There are messages and conversations, comments, and images that have accumulated within us over our lifetimes.

We were taught that certain ladylike, feminine, nurturing, or wanton behavior would bring us success in seeking and/or keeping a mate or finding love. Then we learned we could and should be equal to men in education and career. So we sought higher degrees, more meaningful job selection, and fuller work lives. Still not enough. We had to look beautiful, be as thin as the models on magazine covers, and keep ourselves healthy by having complete Harvard-like knowledge about our bodies, exercise, relaxation techniques, fashion and style, etc.

As babies we learned to smile and be nice and we would get approval. We learned to play nice with our friends, get good grades, keep clean and neat, dress our dolls pretty and we would be praised. So it's natural for us to do what we have to for approval. In the process, we're driving ourselves crazy, feeling empty inside and often lost.

There are solutions. In order to step out away from the abyss and morass of confusion and exhaustion, we must step away, find some time (yes, you can!) for contemplation, look at some options, and make some choices. If you keep running in place, continue draining yourself and dragging yourself down, you will never have time to get healthy because you'll have nothing left. So you must learn to set aside a time period to consider, reevaluate, and work to reach result-oriented decisions.

This process will be made easier by examining basic values. What is important to you? What means the most to you? What gives you the most satisfaction? What are your core beliefs? Who would you be and what would you do at your best with absolute health and maximum energy? Think about values such as family, loyalty, patriotism, love, productivity, creativity, religion, spirituality, integrity, friendship, etc.

Following that step is the scrutiny of your feelings about your values, yourself, your family and your lifestyle. Look at every aspect of your life and check out your feelings: sadness, joy, regret, anger, confusion, pity, satisfaction, frustration, deprivation, jealousy or envy, pride, etc.

The next part can be a lot of fun if you go at it with great enthusiasm and good spirit. It's this: use your imagination and picture your ideal life. Include every part of your life: family, friends, social, spiritual, energy level, health, financial, fashion, recreation, entertainment, travel, study, relaxation, etc. Write this "me chapter" of your life. What do you like to do? Wear? Read? Listen to? Where do you like to go when traveling or when at home? What do you like to watch/see? What makes you happy? Sad? Proud? Depressed? Wondrous? Joyful? Content?

The rest is pretty practical. At this point, you can check out the basic elements necessary for finding balance: finances, education, skills, setting priorities, organization, time charts, action plans, etc.

This semi-final step can also be fun. You've gained some clarity, recognized that you have forced down some once seemingly immovable obstacles, regained some belief in what's possible, and felt some restored vigor and determination. We call this semi-final because it is the next-to-last step. This is the end of the term paper, the last of the research. Take all the facts you have gathered and make a life plan. Put your solutions into your personal life design.

The final step? Live and enjoy.

Take a look at these solutions offered here, and find the ones best suited for your specific behavioral style.

Solutions to life balance:

Hillary

Solution #1: Fuel injection/depletion diagnostic

Yes, you can certainly accomplish more things than most people. You're often proud that you dazzle everyone with the amount of energy you have and how much you can get done in any one day. Do you find that your to-do list is getting longer and your get-up-and-go is feeling more like it's been drained to the last drop? It is time to do a diagnostic test on your energy expenditure – not unlike the kind of run-through mechanics do on your car.

Prepare an inventory of exactly where you are expending your energy in your relationships with yourself and others: work, home, activities, and emotional time (worrying, running in circles, etc.) Don't forget to include your own time for reading, exercising, contemplation, as well as time for fun and entertainment. Assign time values to everything that uses your precious fuel. Add up the time spent and determine your most demanding time and energy drains. Once you have a clear picture of your energy output, you have the information you need to form your energy distribution plan for your life balance.

Inventory of Your Time

Where are you spending your time?	What is it costing you physically and emotionally?

Solution #2: Switch your operation system for introspection

We know it's very hard for you to switch from fast gear to slow, to go from the "doing" mode to the "thoughtful/considering" mode. You are used to flying into action: accomplish, achieve, solve, drive toward your goals. It is easier for you to do things than to sit around contemplating. However, knowing your energy roadmap and keeping the very dear goal in mind of reaching balance in your life, you must recognize the importance of allowing some discomfort from your operating system. Design and schedule time for introspection – for the assessment of your values. Despite your screams of "No Way," we suggest that, at the very least, you take one day off during the week, or a week-end day (or if those are totally out of the question, one full, quiet, night alone) in a place where you will have absolutely no interruptions – and spend time thinking about what you truly care for in life.

What is important to you? Refer to the questions in the last paragraph on page 15. Examine your values. This is not easy. It takes considerable contemplation to escape from your fast-paced, automatic operating mode to being able to recognize the truth about the basic values you actually desire. On the day or evening off, first give yourself some time to simply relax – whether, for you, that is yoga, music, warm bath, meditating, etc. Then think about values, ask yourself questions, write down what you are thinking. Then consider what you've written, and start to reformulate what you really want in life.

Solution #3: Get in touch with your feelings, belief system, and attitudes

Now that you are clearer about your values, it is time to take an even closer look at what's so for you. Right now you're probably feeling the temptation to slam this book down and run back to your normal crazy routine of taking care of the 9,999 things on your list. Take some deep breaths, keep in mind that your goal is to get balance in your life … and force yourself to be still and think. How do you feel (yuck! there's that f—l word again) about the ratio between what you have and where you are in your life, and what your real values are? How have you been programmed to think about deserving what you want in your life? How bad and how fast do you want to get what is important to you? Do you believe you are worthy of getting what you want, and can you be realistic about the things you want? If this is hard at first, just envision what you want your life to be. Get answers to these questions before you can move on.

Solution #4: Make another chart

Okay, now you don't have to think so much. Make a chart of what you decided you want (remember to come from those values you identified) and develop a number system to equate the importance of each. An example might be:

Taking kids to library	8
Exercising on regular basis	5
Cleaning out my jewelry drawer	3
Getting a professional resume done	4
Reconnecting with my old friend	9

Then see how you are designing your actual activity toward these outcomes. See if there is a large disconnect between what is important to you and the amount of energy you expend to accomplish that particular goal. Stop and make a decision about what you want and what you are willing to do to get it.

Solution #5: Get practical

Now that you have a better idea of what you are willing to do to achieve balance in your life, it is time to get results by considering options and making choices. By now, it is abundantly clear that you have a tendency to overwork. Decide if relinquishing some control has a higher value than being in a constant spin in your life. Consider self-employment. Decide from now on that overworking is not an option. Stop making winning the "who gets the most done" contest a high status positive trait. Then ask: do I need additional schooling, do I need to learn more about technology, can I do work at home, can I reduce my work hours, can I freelance, can I go part-time, do I need to learn new skills? Each situation is different. However, considering alternate work styles, different financial options, job sharing, etc. can help us discover solutions to our work/life predicament.

Ivana

Solution #1: Consider what work means to you

Since you are a very social being and enjoy having others around you, a good place for you to start is to gain clarity about what work means for you. Answer questions such as: what role does my work play in my life, what do I expect, what about work brings me happiness and satisfaction, do I have the kind of relationships that I want to have at the job/work I am doing? Are your needs in regard to relationships being met at home or with friends? Or do you need this social activity to be a part of your work? Remember those messages you got when you were younger (and still get in magazines, social interaction, etc.) about being a good girl, being the center of attention, and being popular. Reevaluate those messages and consider them relative to how you are spending your time with family, friends, hobbies, home and personal care, and work.

Solution #2: Use a buddy

Although it's relatively easy for you to express your feelings, it is, however, often uncomfortable for you to be introspective or take quiet time to examine your values and feelings. So for you, a great idea is to enlist the help of another woman. This could be a friend, family member, or co-worker. She may be searching for answers for life balance or perhaps has already experienced finding solutions in this same area. Have her work with you on your likes and dislikes about home and work, what you feel your values are, what worries you about how you spend your time, and what you most deeply care about. You can do this with a question and answer format, or get creative and enlist her help in making it some kind of game. Remember to write down answers. That is very important.

Solution #3: Okay, get serious

You know that at times it is difficult for you to follow through when you can be going out and having a fun time. However, deep down, if you are overworked or unsatisfied with your life balance, perhaps friends and family are giving you messages. This is the time to step up to bat once more to get this self-discovery finished. So, being the social butterfly that you are, use your networking skills. Take some time (you can decide how much time you want to assign to this part of your project, e.g., 2 weeks, 2 months). Every time you are out with individuals or groups in a social setting or work-related networking, let people know you're working on this project, and ask them questions that will give you answers about yourself. For example, ask someone, "Which is more important to you: daily satisfaction at work, or the paycheck?" Have your buddy help you make up some questions designed to give you some information about your values and feelings relative to life issues.

Solution #4: Get out the mixer

After doing the exercises recommended above, you now know the ingredients that are contributing to your life balance dilemma. Throw all of them into a mental mixer or actually write them on scraps of paper and throw them into a bowl. Some examples may be:

"I need to set boundaries at work."

"Since I have so many self-set obligations, these are the ones I can comfortably and temporarily set aside or discard."

"Answering all my e- mails at the end of the day."

"Calling my clients every month."

"Daily coffee break with group."

"Keeping my wardrobe perfectly up to date, i.e., shopping too much."

"Exercising 5 times a week."

Now, pull them out one at a time and give each one a priority number, such as 5-high priority, 4-important, 3-means something to me, 2-I could live without this, and 1-this has got to go. When you are finished with this, all you need is to get into a passionate, enthusiastic state, and design the changes you will make.

Solution #5: Examine alternatives

Create your most realistic ideal situation. You now have such clarity about what is real for you in terms of what you care about, what your own work needs are, and how to eliminate some of the physical and emotional drain you were experiencing. Now, consider some serviceable alternatives. As an example, consider job-sharing, part-time work, changing jobs, returning to school or classes, consulting work, etc. These choices may be helpful as you explore the employment aspects of your time management needs.

Laura

Solution #1: Let's get physical

Having balance in your life is extremely important to you. You can firmly and positively have the awareness that you have structured your life to achieve balance and security. Looking inward is uncomfortable for you. However, you must challenge your comfort zone. This requires that you do a physical inventory. Set aside one or two weeks to do this self-examination. Here's how: when you notice yourself getting upset, when you feel angry, sad, or frightened, put a freeze on yourself – almost as if you're stopping time. Then quickly run a scan on your body to figure out your physical symptoms. Do you have a headache? Do you feel short of breath? Is your chest tight? Do you have stomach discomfort or nausea?

Just be super aware of your physical symptoms when you are having an emotional reaction to a situation.

There is no need to do anything about these physical reactions. Simply observe them and be aware that you are feeling them. You may want to jot these incidents down below, since the next exercise requires you to recall them. You may find this very difficult, as you are unaccustomed to focusing on your own feelings and needs. However, keep your goal in mind. You want to feel secure that your life is working and balanced, and in the end you will be happy.

Solution #2: Reflect

After those two weeks are up (Whew! – was that one of the most difficult things you ever had to do?), take some time to reflect on what you observed about your emotional-physical relationship. Think about what was really going on when you experienced the physical representations of the emotions you were having. Recall what the circumstances were when you experienced these physical responses.

This exercise may be extremely difficult for you because you are not comfortable paying this much attention to yourself. However, if you take this seriously and persevere, you will learn at this point about some long-held beliefs you hold – beliefs that you allow to dictate your behavior in certain situations. For instance, you may observe that, instead of taking an action that would make you feel in alignment with what you want, you sublimate that need and choose another action because you feel compelled to please someone else. After this reflection, you will have some strong clues about choices you make that contribute to imbalance and cause you to feel less than satisfied with your life.

Solution #3: Play the Match Game

Now you are more aware of how the hidden messages stored in your psyche create both physical discomfort and disharmony with your life goals. Make a list of each of the hidden messages or scripts you have used to rule over what you really want. An example may be that you were told by your mother to be a nice girl. Once you begin this process of recalling the messages and beliefs that created the emotional and physical reactions you observed over the past two weeks, it is likely that other "false" beliefs or accepted directives will literally start popping up for you.

Now, match up that thought with the behavior you choose. The message you bought from your parents – that you must be a nice girl – may be represented by accepting a job or task someone asked you to do, because in your mind, doing so means you are being a nice girl. In reality, doing that job ranks #510 on your true priority list. You may set up your list like this:

Hidden Mesage	Behavior
I must be a nice girl	Accepted the filing job at church
If I do things for people, they will like me	Spend one half hour on the phone listening to Julie moan about her miserable marriage
If I go along with the crowd, I will fit in	Attend the fundraiser

Solution #3: Be an author

Take a good look at your list. If you did it correctly, you may have several messages that match the behavior you exhibited during your two-week study.

Now do some rewriting. Get creative. Because you have been so used to letting your established, self-imposed thought programming direct you to take care of others better than you care for your own self, this process may be difficult.

You can approach this with abandon. Remember to keep your goal in mind. You want to create a comfortable and productive balance in your life.

So go for it! Challenge your previously held pseudo beliefs! Cross off "I must be a nice girl" and replace it with what you really want. This may be something like, "I am a good person who makes choices that benefit my health and well-being." Or, instead of "If I do things for people, they will like me," write, "Once I care for my needs and my family's needs, I will be better prepared to contribute to others and my community."

Solution #4: Write your own story

You have gained clarity about what drives you to behave at times in directions and manners that often do not suit your values. Take some time to think about how you would like to behave and what you would like to achieve. If this is too much of a challenge for you, try it this way.

Imagine that you have just been hired as the new writer for a smash, new soap opera. You know the one, It has your name on it. It's called, "_____'s Life." Fill in the blank with your name. Now, outline this soap opera story with how you want to spend your time, where you want to work, how many hours you want to work, how much time you spend being good to yourself promoting your peace of mind, spirituality, physical well-being, with your husband, children, parents, friends, and community. How much time do you want to allocate to fun, planning, vacationing, making money, learning, volunteering, fulfilling your spiritual needs, physical exercise, etc. Once you start answering these questions, you will find it easier to describe ideally how you want to live your life.

Martha

Solution #1: Find the energy sappers

You must challenge your almost automatic modus operandi. We know how important it is for you to do things right. You usually want everything in its place and things done right, preferably the first time. You want order – or dare we say, perfection – even if it means you often feel dissatisfied with life, feel others are getting where you want to be and do not understand why they are there and you are not. Even if it means you are worn down and fighting a feeling of emptiness... that the treadmill you are always on is wearing out.

Well, here's the good part. You know the two or three schedulers or planners you have? In those beautifully organized planners, set aside a day, or if that won't work, at least one half-day, to examine your daily habits. How much time are you spending planning, working, exercising, caring for your family, caring for yourself, worrying, re-organizing, house-cleaning, on the computer, etc? Use your wonderful talent of being orderly to chart the time you spend doing things. You do not have to make any decision at this point. Just chart your activities and times spent.

Energy Sappers

What is draining your energy?	What is it costing you emotionally and/or physically?

Solution #2: Do an attitude check

Remember those messages we got as children? Ask yourself some questions to determine if they are controlling your behavior. Does your work have to be done better than other people do it? Is decision-making difficult for you because you have to get the right answer? Are you the type of person who must be in control? Do unexpected life changes make you uncomfortable? Are you too rigid in your expectations about others or yourself? If it will help, go the library and find a book or look up values, or type in values as your keyword on a computer search. Get an idea of what life values means. Then write down or type up your values. Try to keep your list down to about ten values. Then truly assess your values. How do you feel about things? What is important to you? Since you like order so much, prioritize your list of values.

Solution #3: Assume a persona

It is usually difficult for you not only to express your feelings, but also to identify and acknowledge them. So it's now time for you to play act. It is widely known that many actors are not comfortable or outgoing in everyday life, but they feel very good onstage and can be quite demonstrative when assuming the behavior and traits of a character other than themselves. Ready to give it a try?

First, choose a character – perhaps someone you have seen before: a family member, a character from a book, an actress or TV personality. Choose someone who is overly emotional, always looks neat and attractive, or seemingly free in spirit. Now, take on the cloak of that person. Actually, abandon your rules just for this "play period" and pretend you are that person. This is very tricky because, at this point, you must use the free-ness and emotionality of this character but be honest about your feelings. The purpose of this exercise is to allow yourself to use the carefree behavior and impulsivity of this character to free yourself to look deeply into your own feelings. In the previous exercise, you produced a list of values. Now, you must discover how you feel about those values. As an example, one of your values might be to look perfect. You may feel that in order to be accepted and respected, you must always look perfect. Get in touch with how you feel about your values. Refer back to the start of this chapter on pages 15 and 16 for some examples of feelings.

Solution #4: Outline your objectives

Since you are very comfortable with orderliness and clarity and do not mind working hard, here is a great project for you. You now have a better idea about how you spend your time, what you care about in life, and how you feel about your values. This is a good time to design an outline of your objectives. Here's an example:

Activity	Value	Rank	Feeling	Objective
House cleaning	Order-liness	#17	Gives me sense of balance and clarity, and I feel better when things are in order	Not as important as other priorities, so I will reduce time spent to only 5 hours/week
Spending time with friends	Friend-ship	#7	Sense of belong-ing, sharing, being social	Even though my expectations have limited close rela-tionships, I want to join some new groups, and get out one night/week for a class and once/month on a 'date' with a friend

Solution #5: Become powerful with a formal life creation

Here is a true opportunity to regain power over your life. Instead of compulsive or forced behavior about your daily routines, now you have the chance to set up how you want your life to look, feel, and be. Here is your shot at using logic, which has always been so important to you, to put together a life plan. Using all the information you have gathered from the previous exercises - plus anything you may not have had in your life prior to this self-exploration, such as travel, massages, financial planning, a certain style of dressing, or spirituality – design how you would like your life to look to please you, not others. Formally write out your new life plan.

Solution #6: Set boundaries, consider your options, and get a good proverbial "bookshelf"

In order to make your life plan work, you must now consider practicality and options. For instance, to decrease the amount of time you spend at work, one option would be to change your function within your company. You may be able to take on a role that is equally enjoyable, but less demanding. Other choices could be telecommuting, home offices, job sharing, etc. Another example of what you may have learned from the previous exercises is that you can do less now. For instance, you now know that much of what was so time-consuming was that you had a hard time saying no, or you were not willing to limit what you thought you wanted to accomplish. Now you have decided to say "yes" when your high-priority values are involved, and "no" when the value involved is a lower priority for you. Or, "it wasn't my work culture that set my standards; it was me" and now, " I don't have to be the one that has the best presentation for every project."

About that proverbial "bookshelf." Take some of those activities that you successfully identified as having a lower priority value for you, and put them on your bookshelf to pick up later, maybe next year. At another time, you may get to those lower-priority activities on your bookshelf. Perhaps it will be after that important job change, or after you've started your at-home business, or now that you are spending less time at work and more time volunteering with your daughter's class or at the home for the elderly. Once you feel more comfortable about your life balance, you will be able to accomplish more while feeling better, and soon will be able to get to those bookshelf things in your life.

~three~

Health

"If you have your health, you have everything."

How often have you heard some variation of that statement? We are supposed to realize on a daily basis how fortunate we are if we have good health. However, that rarely is the case. It takes a September 11 event, a death, or a close call with a life-threatening illness or catastrophe for us to get back in touch with the realization that our health is basic, and the most important ingredient in the success of living our lives.

Just as a middle school or high school youngster fails to connect the effect of drug use on her personal consequences, we keep ourselves automatically operating as if our personal health were a condition that someone – a neighbor or a fictional character in a book – has to be concerned with; not us. The thought of our health is buried somewhere, maybe deep at the back of our necks, or some vague discomfort in our gut. However, most often it is thought of as "I'll deal with it at some unforeseen, whenever I get to it, date in the future."

Why is that? Great question. However, it does not beg an easy answer.

One woman we know had a father who made it quite clear that if she stayed in bed when she felt ill, she was somehow a "baby" or she was only "pretending." She got real brownie points when she went to school feeling rotten, whether with heavy cold or flu symptoms or severe stomach cramps. She learned well that it wasn't important to take care of herself. However, she sure learned that taking care of others was important.

She got rave reviews for that.

So, growing up female, we get the message that taking care of ourselves is somehow wrong. Or, it's only okay when we get permission from our husband or doctor to produce the justification that we require. We are very willing – no matter what state we're in – to take care of our children, husbands, parents, bosses, employees, aunts, pets, etc. We are great at delaying – and sometimes readily marvel out loud how overdue we are at getting - health tests or seeing a doctor about a problem we've been having. Often we abdicate responsibility for our own self-care, and sometimes allow ourselves to get out of control, because we keep thinking about how unfair it is that we have so much to do – instead of taking action to change how we think and behave.

In order for us to truly function, we must pay attention to our health. Without it, we lack pizzazz, vitality, and life energy. So often women walk around feeling exhausted, out of control, and as if we have just been knocked out by Muhammad Ali.

Some symptoms of sickness can include fatigue, headaches, neck aches, high blood pressure, being under weight, being overweight, muscle pains, gastro-intestinal problems and pain, skin rashes or irritations, heart palpitations, problems with sleeping or breathing, dizziness, biting nails or lips, feet or leg problems, crying often, chronic sadness or temper tantrums, taking drugs, smoking cigarettes, alcohol abuse, debilitating worry, etc.

Being healthy is spiritual, mental, and physical well-being. To be healthy, women must get enough sleep, proper nourishment and adequate exercise; see a doctor regularly for check-ups and keep stress to a moderate level; have opportunities for rest, relaxation and recreation; be able to laugh and enjoy a sense that life is good and right.

Most importantly, women must realize that their attitude is supreme when it comes to being healthy. Commitment, action and follow-through come next.

Please stop now and ask yourself these questions:

• Am I ready to believe that good health is vital to all aspects of my life, including happiness and success?

- Am I willing to develop the right attitude to create my good health?

- Am I ready to transform the state of my health to its optimal level?

- Am I ready to make the commitment necessary to be as healthy as I need to be?

- Am I ready to take the necessary action, and to continue with the appropriate follow-through, to complete this goal?

If you answered "yes" to any of the questions above, know that there are steps and processes you can follow to become as healthy as possible. By using our behavioral styles to guide you, you can learn the solutions and follow the recommendations in this chapter to feel better, look better, and enjoy your life with more ease and intensity. A su salud! A votre santé! Alla vostra salute! Zu Ihrer Gesundheit!

Solutions to Health Issues:

Hillary

Solution #1: Viewpoint exam

Stop the madness, frenzy, and must-do activities for one moment, and ask yourself the following question: "Do I want to wait until after a heart attack, an emotional or mental breakdown of some sort, or some health-related catastrophe to examine my willingness to be aware of my physical and mental state?" You probably feel you can't afford the time to be concerned about your health because you are working on things to get the results that are important to you right this moment. You've got clothes to wash, stock portfolios to check, kids to take to soccer games, or proposals to get done by their deadlines. Will you stop and check your calendar, and schedule in one annual doctor's exam? Can you perceive doing that as valid for the ultimate result: you continuing to be healthy enough to get all that you need to get done – done, while you are either healthy enough or still here to do them?

Solution #2: Body scan

Now that you have begrudgingly accepted the realization that you are not

immune to being exhausted or getting ill, perhaps you will do an examination of a different sort. Going to the doctor may help if you are already ill. But aggravating physical symptoms that often bother us at home or at work may be problems resulting from decisions we make, such as what we choose to eat, what kind of exercise we get, how many hours of sleep we get, or how much stress we allow in our lives. So for a day or so, physically check yourself out. Do you have any neck pain? Do your shoulders hurt? Having any bellyaches, discomfort, headaches or chest tightness? Do your feet hurt? Do you have any eye problems? Do you have any problems sleeping or eating? Are you crying or yelling often? You like to be in control. So take control of your physical symptoms.

Solution #3: Become Zelda Freud

In the exercise above, you've taken inventory of your physical symptoms. Let's take a closer look at your psychological symptoms. Do you find yourself feeling guilty for any number of reasons, such as neglecting family or friends, not completing the gazillion tasks you have begun, or because you are not living up to the extreme expectations you have set for yourself? Do you often feel overloaded or super fatigued? Are you finding fault with others too easily, or feeling more and more isolated? Do you feel tense, pressured, as if you literally feel the weight of the world on your shoulders? Do you feel as if you cannot stop running or are dragging all the time? Do you feel resentful of others, with the sense that no one understands you? Do you feel as if you can't catch up or want to run away? Check yourself carefully for any of these telling symptoms and write them down.

Solution #4: Draw up blueprints for results

Women today find themselves in situations in which setting limits is extremely difficult. In fact, you most likely are inspired and energized by the rush of adrenaline that surges through you when you juggle the seemingly hundreds of activities, demands, responsibilities, phone conversations, e-mails, memos, meetings, events, committees, etc. that you may handle on a daily basis. You can still enjoy an active, high-energy home, work, and social life without the accompanying symptoms of pain and discomfort you may have discovered from your body scan during your previous exercise. Make a chart of the discoveries you have made and alongside the symptoms, jot down some possible solutions for these revealing signals of portending or existing health problems.

Symptom	Possible Options
Back pain	Doctor visit, chiropractor, exercise
Not wanting to get out of bed in the morning	Talk with a friend, do yoga, eliminate one activity per day
Picking fights at work and with my husband	Talk to my husband, talk with a counselor, develop signal device to control my temper before I release it
Nagging headache	Medication, meditation, jotting down the time the headaches are worse, doctor visit

Solution #5: Hop to it

It has most often been your style to make quick decisions. Most women tend to talk themselves out of checking themselves out, health-wise. After making your chart (above) do not contemplate, consider, or attempt to weigh the pros and cons of the options. Take your chart and read each option one time, and one time only. Now, using a red pen or marker, without thinking, underline the first option that you are drawn to. Quickly go to your computer, your yellow legal pad, or whatever writing paper you find most comfortable. Make two columns: In one write down the pain or discomfort and in the other column, the one option. Leave space between each row. Under the rows, write down the words Action, When, and Numbers. Fill in the spaces for Action, When, and Numbers with what you will do to follow through with the option, when you will do it, and phone numbers or e-mail addresses to order to get the job done.

Symptom	Possible Options
Back pain	Chiropractor
Action: Make an appointment **When:** Call tomorrow morning, 9:00 a.m. **Number:** 999-999-9999	
Not wanting to get out of bed in the morning	Eliminate one activity per day
Action: Review monthly calendar and cross off one activity for each day **When:** Thursday morning, 4/05, 8-9 a.m	
Picking fights at work and with my husband	Develop signal device to control my temper before I release it
Action: Get book on this subject at library, read, choose device, use and review results **When:** Friday evening, 4/06, 7:00 p.m.	

With your style and the systems for living you have built for yourself, it may be quite difficult to find or make time for whatever spirituality you choose. Spirituality basically comes down to finding meaning in life, however one packages that in belief. So, this is a personal decision for you, and yet it can only cause disease and difficulties if it is not addressed. You must decide on a form of mindfulness for you to get in touch with your inner self. You may choose gardening, experiencing this process during yoga, listening to music, or just taking ten – only ten – minutes at times to practice concentrated breathing. The reward for you will be greater than whatever task, assignment, or accomplishment that you may be tempted to do during that ten minutes. Perhaps a quiet romantic dinner at an outdoor café with your significant other or a special friend, a run down a hill feeling the sunshine and wind, or a walk in the forest – find a way that you enjoy for some solitude and introspection.

Ivana

Solution #1: Check out the view

Give yourself an assignment for about five days. When you are at work, involved in a charitable or social event, spending time with your pals, or

doing daily chores, look around you and notice other women. Who looks happy, who looks successful, full of energy, ready to take on the next challenge? Who looks tired and dragging, worn-out, pale, fidgety, or as if she were in pain? You will start to get a very good sense about physical, mental, and spiritual health. If you feel comfortable, you can discuss your assignment with others. You will begin to see that in order for your life to function, you must have good health.

Solution #2: Do a pal poll

Since you are a people-person and enjoy sharing your life so much with others, the best way for you to get an accurate picture of your state of health, both emotionally and physically, is to talk with your friends. In fact, take a poll. Go back to the introduction of this chapter, and review some of the symptoms listed. Then actually make your own list and ask others if they perceive you as having any of those symptoms, or if you have been complaining about any of those symptoms. Sometimes we go unconscious and don't even register in our own memory some of the problems we mention to others from time to time. Make up questions such as:

- "Have I said anything lately about having headaches, stomachaches, or any other bodily aches of any kind that you can recall?"

- "Have I appeared moody, or sad, or more difficult to get along with than usual?"

- "Have I shown any signs of unusual nervousness, irritability, or fatigue more than I usually do?"

Make up about ten questions. Then ask away. The trick here is that you must entrust yourself to really listen to what your friends and family have to say. Not only listen, but also write down what they tell you. Then read it over several times.

Solution #3: Self-diagnosis

At this point, you have answers about your physical and mental state of being. Review the answers you have gotten from your poll. Now take time to think about the answers you received. Think about what hits home for you. What comes across the page loud and clear as you reread what you've written? Do you exhibit more signs of physical pain or discomfort, or does it seem clear that you are demonstrating results of overload or stress? If you feel that the results are not crystal clear, this time pick one family member or friend, and have her help you get clear about what you have been told. It is very possible that you have multi-symptoms of ill health, and it means you must interpret the results.

Solution #4: Interpret

Write down your results, using the form below, to determine what may be causing some of these challenges. Decide, as best you can from the comment, which is the appropriate category for that possible illness.

Who Said It?	Mary
What did she say?	I always complain about being tired

Physical		Emotional/Psychological	Spiritual
X	or	X	

Who Said It?	Amy
What did she say?	I often complain about stomachaches

Physical	Emotional/Psychological	Spiritual
X		

Who Said It?	Reggie
What did she say?	I seem to be angry a lot

Physical	Emotional/Psychological	Spiritual
	X	

After you have written all this down, add up your marks and see if you see certain patterns. Now it is time to prioritize.

Solution #5: Point and appoint

Determine what categories your symptoms point to and add them up to see where is the best place to start. Naturally, if you have more physical symptoms, call your doctor. That is most likely the best first step to make. Tell her about your symptoms so she can determine what tests or care is

required. Later, you can determine if you require visits with other doctors, relaxation exercises, a vacation, more physical activity, more sleep, going on a shopping spree, examining some relationships or some other solution.

Here's an additional hint that may aid you in this process. With your personality style, it is possible that you'll want to tell everyone who will listen what you have discovered about your health at this time. Just for now, until you have a firm hold on what exactly is causing your symptoms and what is the best action to take, restrict yourself to one family member and one friend. Choosing to do this may enhance the energy necessary for you to restore to a stronger state and not dissipate your power to formulate the best course of action.

Solution #6: Make sure you get back to home base

Using a baseball analogy, if you hit the ball hard and start running the bases, but somehow do not return to home base, you will not score. You can do all the hard work, get instructions from a doctor, and even start a plan. However, if you do not have a system to guarantee follow-through, your accomplishments may not take you to completion of your goal. Now you can enlist help from others. Get suggestions from doctors, clergy, friends, co-workers, teachers, etc. and develop a consistent, workable plan.

It could be something as simple as listing steps you will take – being very specific about when, how, where, and with whom – or keeping stickers on a calendar, making a poster to keep in a place where you will see it every day, or any technique to ensure you keep on your path to good health. Once you have done that, perhaps enlist the help of someone you trust to help ensure your successful follow-through with these exercises, practices, and goals.

Laura

Solution #1: Take your temperature

With your personality, it is not uncommon for you to stuff your problems down or divert your attention to others instead of looking at your own situation. Therefore, for the sake of your health and for those who love you, you must, if necessary, force yourself to take your temperature by assessing your mood, your sense of well being, your enjoyment of life, the quality you experience in your life every day, and your energy level. Give yourself one week to check yourself out, truly observe how you are feeling and behaving. Use the health thermometer below or create some standards of your own, and rate your health. When you stop to think about these matters, you can come up with ideas of your own to make this an even more personal assessment.

Use a marking scale for the questions below, ranging from a #1 being pretty jaunty and seeing the rosy side of things to #5, which is, "Call the ambulance." See the results you get from this personal health quiz.

Behavior	Score
1. Do I look forward to getting out of bed in the morning?	_____
2. Do I feel as if others are taking advantage of me?	_____
3. Do I feel agitated and worried a lot?	_____
4. Do I secretly feel sorry for myself?	_____
5. Do I have headaches, chest tightness, or any other physical symptom on a regular basis?	_____
6. Am I smoking or drinking too much?	_____
7. Do I feel tired often?	_____
8. Do I bite my nails, overeat, or regularly have a nervous habit?	_____
9. Do I often think others are happier or having more fun than me?	_____
10. Do I feel lost, left out, have a feeling that I'm not getting anywhere?	_____

Add all your answers. If you scored 30 or below, you are doing well, and you may have discovered a few specific areas that need tending. If you scored above 30, you may have to consider more serious attention to your overall physical and psychological condition.

Solution #2: Check the scale

Yes, you can get on the scale and make sure that your weight is well within the range of safety for your height and body type. However, here we are referring to all-around measurements for some sound health habits to see where you fit. Are you drinking enough water? Are you eating your fruits and vegetables? Do you get enough exercise? Do you get to the doctor once a year for your physical exam? Do you stay informed about health-related issues? Are you getting enough sleep and rest? Do you include stress-reducing activities in your life? Do you like yoga and meditation? Are you still making sure you include these kinds of activities in your schedule weekly? Now that you've measured these health habits, plan to change one habit per week or per month so you're happy with your health scale.

3. Solution #3: An attitude check

In addition to paying attention to physical symptoms and habits, it is a good idea to get to the core of your own attitudes about your own health. You have a tendency to worry and can be fearsome at times. However, by being more concerned for the welfare of others, you know that you may neglect yourself. Do you believe you accept and value yourself? Do you feel that your life, health, and happiness are your responsibility? Do you believe it is important to pay attention to the dispensation of your energy? Do you, deep in your heart, realize that in order to prevent self-harm, you must know the answers to these questions, and must keep conscious about your health and how you maintain it? Carefully think about these questions, formulate your answers, and commit to doing whatever is necessary to remain healthy – for your own sake as well as for others who love you.

4. Solution #4: Tell the truth about your excuses

You probably have thought about your health in the past and as you look back, have you made excuses about keeping your health commitments? Excuses such as: I don't have time, by the time I can exercise, it's too late and I'm too tired, I don't have time to plan healthy meals, I always lose my water bottle, etc., etc. Friends, work, kids, volunteering – all these things are reasons for you to neglect yourself and let your health slide, right? Make an excuse list. Sit down and think about all the excuses you have used to not eat healthy, to not get enough rest, to let yourself get stressed out, to not exercise, to overeat, etc., etc. Get out that pen and journal, and list all the excuses you can remember. Now, write down the truth about that excuse, and develop a plan to do what you have to do to restore your well-being.

5. Solution #5: Socially happy

Talk to a best friend or a few good friends and suggest that you form a health club. You can do all kinds of projects in this club. Some examples are:

• Plan regular walks together.

• Exchange healthy-food recipes.

• Assign different women's health issues or medical problem to one another, look up information about the issue or problem at the library or on the internet, and report what you have discovered to each other.

• Babysit while the others go to doctor appointments, or if no kids are involved, commit to go on appointments with your friend(s). Lunch at a special restaurant before or after wouldn't hurt.

• Gift one another with surprise stress busters (neck massages, small basket of fruit, pedicures, a new book or tape on yoga, pilates, or meditation, etc.).

• Book a spa day together as a reward after awhile of good health and supporting one another.

• Come up with your own promises and ideas to support health amongst you.

Martha

Solution #1: Conduct your own study

Since you are most often conscientious about most aspects of your life, you most likely are eating properly and getting the proper amount of exercise. However, life has so much stimuli and demands for women today, and it is likely that within your busy existence, you may not consider a clear view of the effect of stress on your health. There is definitely a steady amount of stress in our daily lives. However, over-stress may happen when some other-than-normal occurrence happens in your life, such as a death, divorce, loss of job, or some threat to what one considers normal in one's life. Over-stress may also be the result of something positive such as a celebration, a new career position, marriage, etc. Use your local bookstore, the library, or the internet to get facts on what is considered stress or over-stress. Gather all the information and see how your physical shape and feelings, sleeping patterns, moods, and other symptoms match up with the knowledge you gain from this study.

Solution #2: Take a trip

Now that you have all that information, and have been your usual logical self, it may be necessary at this point to stray a bit from your natural inclinations. You might have to step aside from your logical approaches, just for a brief time. We'll ask you to use your normal analytical style in a moment. However for now, we would like you to make a serious attempt at being intuitive. Using your powers of concentration combined with a more free-style approach, start at the top of your head and work your way down to your toes, travel inside and outside your body, and ask yourself how are you feeling and how, for a while, you have been feeling. It is helpful to put aside about one hour to do this exercise, and even better to play some soft relaxing music while you do it. Don't bother writing anything down at this time. Just travel, relax, and notice what your body is telling you.

Solution #3: Write it yourself

We might suggest to others that they look on the internet, check out magazines, or find books with written tests that determine your state of health or well-being. However, with your personality type, you would do best to write your own assessment. You have a high standard for quality and will construct a good evaluation about your level of health. You have the knowledge you gathered from resources in the first exercise above, and the information you ascertained from your travel through your own body. Using all you have learned from those assessments, construct a self-test.

Remember to cover all aspects of being healthy. Include general feeling, ability to enjoy yourself, feelings of being strong, feelings of joyfulness or lack of it, fatigue, aches, pains, eyesight, hearing, limbs, smoking habits, eating habits, etc. Then construct a rating system and grade yourself on your state of health.

Solution #4: Be Prepared

Review your values from Chapter Two. Remind yourself that you must be well in order to do your best work, take care of family, and enjoy your hobbies. Evaluate what you discovered from your self-test. Now, you must be prepared to make a commitment to do whatever is necessary to restore yourself to your best physical and mental health. That usually involves medical check-ups by your gynecologist, eye doctor, internist, and even your dentist. Your commitment may involve planning health breaks, small weekend trips to relax, reassessing your fitness program, joining a support group, or reinvigorating a special diet. Use your strong sense of organization, and develop a health plan.

Solution #5: Hit the ball, water the plants, go the next day to the gym …

You wouldn't stop at getting your tennis racket up in the air for a good, hard smack of that tennis ball, and then not hit it and follow through with your swing … or plant your garden and not water your plants … or start an exercise program and only go once to the gym. The same is true with your health plan – you must follow through! You've done the research, you developed a test, you took and graded your test, you recommitted to being healthy, and now you must follow through. You enjoy taking time to evaluate consequences. So, take the time to follow through with your plan by making appointments, filling your calendar with reminders throughout the year, and creating monthly activities to keep yourself fit, strong, and happy.

~four~
Relationships
Family, Friends & Associates

Honest, complete connection with another person.

Close your eyes for a moment and travel through your mind's eye. Recall a time in your childhood when you were having a peaceful yet stimulating discussion with someone.

Can you remember talking about issues truly important to your soul – and then immediately thinking, "this feels so good" or "this is so right"? Can you remember that amazing discovery; that wonderful sense of connection ... the feeling that being with this person was so right? Can you remember thinking the experience felt like a reality beyond what had previously felt normal? What the experience represents is relating honestly and completely with someone; that is, having a relationship.

Actually, that's a description of a pretty special and happy relationship. The opposite could be true, and most women likely have experienced it — the screaming, shrieking, out of control exchange of anger and vitriolics that characterizes a disturbing, defective relationship.

Having loving, healthy, and nourishing relationships in our lives is almost as vital as our basic survival needs. Healthy relationships equal the fulfillment of needs between two or more people. There are many kinds of relationships. We have them with self, the opposite sex, friends, family, work associates, etc. We will explore relationships with romantic partners in our chapter on love and sex. This chapter deals with all other types of relationships.

The degree of success we have in our relationships is dependent on many factors, such as how we were raised, our personalities and beliefs, expectations, behavior, and health. We'll explore these components with the objective of identifying the kinds of relationships you seek, the development and maintenance of those relationships, the threats of certain kinds of relationships, the positive effects of your relationships, and some tips for enhancing your relationships.

There are some elements about relationships that are specific to women. Women, to a great degree, have been raised to be nurturers. So we put great stock in being good at our role in relationships. Therefore, it is not surprising that women care a great deal about the success of those relationships. Men may emphasize other aspects, such as sports or career achievements.

You have probably heard the common fabrication that women are not nice to one another and may be rather nasty to one another. This myth may be a carry-over from adolescent jealousies. Most women are characteristically caring and supportive of one another.

Women also have generally had very high standards regarding relationships. However, at times, we put up with more guff than would be wise to withstand. Just as the old song refrain has told us to "stand by your man," we've been taught to stay true to a friend through thick and thin – or even mistreatment. There's a solid reason to limit standing by your friend, if a toll is being taken on you.

Relationships at work have their own inherent difficulties for women. Not that long ago, it was thought that the workplace was no place for women, especially after they had children. Some people still feel that way today. Women were unsure whether to act like a man to fit in and get ahead, or to be the demure lady and hope to somehow get recognition. Getting along with one's boss or work peers is an imposing challenge by itself, without the mantle of being the obliging woman in an old boys network. In addition, there has been the added indignity of sexual advances and harassment.

Another added complication is the media model presented to women in movies, magazines, TV and music. Not only have women been made to feel that they have to be great moms and wives, super sexy, model thin, and aggressive, successful career women – but we must also be good pals, unselfish, and other-centric in our relationships. Here once again, we have been prodded to be everything to everybody.

The important point to focus on about relationships is that creating a positive connection with another person brings many benefits and pleasures in our lives. So now let us take a look at your particular style of behavior as it relates to your relationships with family, friends, social acquaintances, and school, work, or church associates. Let's explore the state of your relationships: whether to hang on to them for dear life or discard them as fast as you can fling them; how much they do or don't mean to you; and what if anything you want to do about them.

Solutions to relationship problems:

Hillary

Solution #1: Review your connections

It is no secret to you that having control is key, and the importance of control has an influence on your relationships. Relationships you make and maintain are usually with other high achievers or those who share similar goals of mutual benefit. For the most part, you are motivated by results, which unfortunately, at times, inhibits the development of friendships.

Ask yourself honestly whether at some rare, but reflective times, you've noticed that you have a small number of relationships, or that the ones you have are not as fulfilling as you would like, or that on some occasions you would like greater support. You may discover that you would like to improve or increase the number of your relationships. If you could slow down and relax your drive for a while, there are ways to do this within your personality style.

Solution# 2: Examine the roles

There are some people (your authors among them) who believe that those with whom we have relationships serve different roles in our lives. Some people make us feel loved and cherished. Others may serve as our counselors. Some relationships make us feel needed, some are fun, some bring out our strengths, and some help us raise our capabilities and accomplishments or build trust. Take a look at those with whom you currently share relationships, i.e. parents, children, co-workers, social acquaintances, etc. See if you have too many of one kind of relationship and too little of others. See if you wouldn't want to balance those scales a little differently. Make a list of the relationships you have. Next to each person's name (excluding spouse or mate for now), write down the roles you think you have with one another.

Example:

Joan – Needer – always wants me to make her feel better, solve her problems

Diane – Sharer – most often she and I just have a great time together

Mom – Guilt provider – almost every time I talk with her, I feel guilty about something

Solution #3: Throw out the dysfunctional relationships

You have very high standards for yourself and for others. So in making judgments about your relationships, first ensure that you are considering carefully whether your expectations are level, whether you are too self-motivated or selfish and thus not allowing for a true two-way relationship, or whether you are solely focused on your own goals. Now, review your list and see if some relationships are less than fulfilling, wasteful of your time and energy, creating feelings of obligation rather than mutual trust and respect, or in your honest opinion, just plain rotten. For now, however, let's take a look at some of your behaviors and see if what you are doing may be spoiling the connections a little.

Solution #4: Is it me?

Consider some important criteria for successful relationships. How do you rate yourself in these areas?

• Am I available when a friend needs me?

• Do I take the time to listen when a friend would like to unload?

• Do I call back friends when they call – or soon enough?

• Do I follow up on suggestions to go out together by checking my calendar or offering definite dates?

- Do I follow through and ask about outcomes when I know something is important to a friend, such as a job interview, meeting a new fellow, kid's recital, etc?

- Do I share my important happenings with my friends?

- Do I keep an opposing viewpoint to myself when I know it would stir up some bad feelings between us?

- Do I constantly chatter about what's going on in my life?

- Am I often complaining, being negative, focusing on the downside of things?

- Am I often crabby? Am I too often fretting out loud?

- Do I try to "fix something" whenever a friend tells me something instead of just listening?

- Do I overly brag about my husband? Children? Job? Looks? Possessions?

- Am I too serious and forget to just have fun or laugh about things?

- Am I forgiving about minor normal infractions?

- Do I expect too much of my friends?

- Do I give credence to my friends' points of view?

- Am I more concerned about being right than being a friend?

- Do I encourage a friend to take a risk, to work harder at something that would likely improve a situation that has been holding her back, or take the time to brainstorm with her about it?

- Am I too rigid about punctuality, keeping appointments, wanting to choose the same type of way to spend time together?

- Do I hide my feelings too much and demand a superficiality with my relationships?

- Do I ever think to buy my friend a little "just thinking of you" card or gift?

- Do I insist that my friends maintain my energy level?

- When I meet someone I like, do I send signals that I would like to begin a relationship?

- Do I take the time to strike up a conversation with that nice person at the gym, the one I often see at work in the rest room, the one who seems so pleasant in the morning coffee line, etc?

- Do I go to classes, workshops, bookstores, and other places where I might meet someone with mutual interests or values?

- Do I take the time to think or say I am grateful for a relationship?

Solution #5: Tweaking Time

You have taken a look at the number and nature of your relationships, and your role in determining the success of your relationships. Before you continue, be aware that at about this point you are probably becoming impatient. You feel you do not have time for this. After all, you have things to do. However, this is precisely the time to "suck it up" and finish what you started.

Consult your list of how you and your friends interact, and notice if the roles each are playing satisfies the needs of both people. See if the roles fit well or need to be adjusted. Then evaluate both sets of answers: what roles my friends are playing, and how am I as a friend. At this point, you are ready to decide which relationships are perfect or need minor or major adjustments – and what you are willing to do about it. Now is the time to decide what books you will read, or if you want to talk with a counselor or make some revelations to your friends because of what you discovered about your own role as a friend. Tweak, tweak, tweak. However, in some cases tweaking is not the answer. With those relationships, the rotten, smelly ones, you must be courageous and find a way to end them.

Solution #6: Make friends with your family

We often get advice from psychologists that we are not to be friends with our children. Although many of us are good friends with our parents, we do not often think in terms of being friends with our mothers and fathers. Whether friends or not – family members are people with whom you have a relationship. We must raise our children, and then give them the gift of letting go. We must obey our parents, and then go off and live our lives as responsible adults. There are so many interactions between those boundaries. So it is actually much better, and creates a more positive environment all around, when we treat our family like we treat our friends.

Since you most often have a direct approach, it may be possible that you do not always treat your family members as friends. It is interesting that we often treat those we love the most with less respect or consideration than we would a friend or acquaintance. We assume our family will accept us as we are. Sometimes "as we are" is somewhat offensive.

Take a look at your relationship with your family members in a way similar to the exercises you did above with your friends. See if you are too demanding of your children since you have such high expectations for yourself and others. Can you give a little more slack? See if you can be a bit more flexible with your folks. Can you demonstrate a little more care about what's going on in their lives? It is true that you have a fear of losing control or being taken advantage of. See if you can overcome those fears by coming from their point of view once in awhile, by being a little less impatient with them, and by finding some time or small way to let them know how much you care for them.

Solution #7: Just because we work together doesn't mean I want to be your friend

Think about the amount of time you spend with the people you work with. That's a lot of time. So it's very important that you consider the types of relationships you have with your work colleagues. It may be a good idea to make a quick list of the kinds of people you would like to be around, such as people who are direct, who take orders well, results-oriented, idea-producers, etc., and the kinds of people you prefer not to be around, such as smokers, detail-oriented people, analyzers, etc. Then, see what you can do about sticking close to those you prefer and avoiding others whenever possible.

Even though you may not want to socialize at work, you want to be aware of your behavior. Conflict is okay. Realize that you cannot always have control or the last word, that others are going to look at things differently, and that varying viewpoints are okay and in many cases productive. Remember: you cannot always work alone, and you may have to share parts of a project. Accept that some people want to think about things before they take immediate action. Be prepared to adjust to those kinds of situations so that work relationships do not become war zones.

Ivana

Solution #1: Erase some lines

If you were looking at a picture of your life and relationships, and the people in your life were dots, there would be far more lines drawn than white areas. As you know, you are a people person. You put a lot of value on relationships. They are important to you. You may be why the word "schmoozing" was invented. Does this suggest that some imbalance may exist? Perhaps. You may want to examine your motives for some of your associations. Do you genuinely like the person with whom you have this relationship? Or, do you feel she builds you up by her status? You might want to reevaluate the nature of some of your relationships, and consider reducing the number that you foster, if they get in the way of your ability to be self-disciplined or if they create conflict with accomplishing your goals. You can use the same process as Hillary in her Solution #2.

Solution #2: Tighten those loose lips

Because you have such high energy around people, because approval is so important to you, and because you express your feelings so openly, it will most likely be to your advantage to take a closer look at your interaction with your friends. Do you reveal too much about your feelings? Do you put yourself in a position in which the information you impart can be used as fodder by people who actually do not have your best interests at heart? Often what you think is what comes out of your mouth. As women, we often say to ourselves with the best of intentions that we are going to do something. However, especially with your personality type, follow-through often does not happen. Therefore, some your friends will not take you very seriously about your plans. This can be very uncomfortable because you feel you are very sincere. It's a good idea to check yourself before you spill forth in social situations.

Solution #3: Question your membership in the club

If you find yourself responding in a relationship because you will maintain your popularity or status with a group, you may consider renewing your membership in that particular club. Because approval is so important to you, you may be doing things that are not comfortable for you just to remain accepted within a group. Does that sound possible? At social functions and when in the process of developing your relationships, if someone is unkind or critical, or they ignore or use you, you may want to find another place to fill this need. In this circumstance, you want to be self-protective. Monitor what you say and do, and be aware of readily available steps to take. If you are not being true to who you really are, these could become disturbing relationships.

Solution #4: Be your own internal camera

The best way to develop a technique to monitor what you are saying and how your words may be interpreted is to think back over past conversations. See if you can recall being bored or having to listen to someone longer than you would have preferred. Then, observe yourself from this point on, and see if you can catch certain phrases or comments that you make to encourage these types of interactions. You are spontaneous, and will be able to think of a socially acceptable way to withdraw from that situation.

Solution #5: Use your common grounds

You never do as well or feel completely comfortable working alone. The key to your success is collaboration. Collaborate at home, with friends, at work, whenever and wherever possible. You will always accomplish more that way. That means focusing on the goals of others as well as having others focused on your needs. This will help you at work. Since you have a tendency to be disorganized in some situations, this solution will assist you by having others catch areas to keep things more in order for you. By keeping this solution in mind at work, you can improve group projects, direct others toward more successful strategies and, by asking the right questions, direct your boss or co-workers to solve problems.

Solution #6: Let's get serious, serious

You tend to be outgoing and value relationships more than goals and accomplishments. That doesn't mean there aren't dreams you earnestly want to fulfill. It just means that in actuality, those end results often do not materialize. You may also influence your children or friends with your carefree, "let's party" attitude. So enlist the assistance of those around you to take a more serious approach, to help you gain more discipline, and to keep you focused on accomplishing what you say you want to do. You might ask someone in your family or a friend to set a definite time to examine and list your goals with you. You might ask someone to check up on you at certain intervals to see if you are following through. Make mutual commitments with others to develop a type of behavior you want to improve your life.

An example would be, "Let's owe one another $1.00 for every time I am late, and you eat a piece of candy." If you know you will have to lay out cash when you've given in to a habit you dislike, it may motivate you to behave differently.

Another possibility could be, "I'll remind you when you are getting way too angry, if you help me set up my budget."

When you make efforts to be less loose, you may influence your family members and others with whom you have relationships to take you more seriously. It may also result in you making greater efforts to be more disciplined.

Solution #7: Don't jump off that bridge

You are often motivated by status, and have concentrated so much on winning people to your side that you make too big a connection between your status and your own self-esteem. We've all heard this motherly admonishment to her child: "If everyone else jumped off a bridge, would you jump too?"

Since one of your fears is rejection, you may be behaving like that child. Take a moment and reflect on some habits you have developed. Are they behaviors you would have chosen if not motivated to have people like or approve of you? Do you want others to like you so much that you let your better judgment take control? If your answer is "yes," then you may want to reread Chapter One and do some of the exercises. You need to get a stronger picture of your self-worth, and break the connection between the value you place on yourself and the approval you get from others.

Laura

Solution #1: Re-focus

Relationships do a lot for our state of being. They can motivate us, inspire us, foster self-acceptance, and bring us fun, comfort, and joy. These rewards are great, providing our relationships are structured to create these results.

But since you may have a tendency to not "rock the boat" and you tend to be nice to influence others to like you, your relationships may not be producing the highest quality results. Often-heard advice for being a good friend is to tell someone to stop focusing on herself and to think about the other person's feelings and needs. However, you might do well to refocus your viewpoint on yourself. With your behavioral style that seeks to find solutions to please everyone, to avoid conflict, or to cooperate in most situations, you may sacrifice the benefits of your relationships. Take a look at your relationships, and begin to think about their dynamics. How do friends treat you? Do you give in too much at work? Are your needs overlooked in your relationships?

Solution #2: Record your findings

Now that you have considered the nature of your relationships, you may want to confirm what you have discovered by keeping a record. Plan on observing your relationships for a month or two, and actually keep a record of the exchanges in those important relationships. It could be as simple as writing the name of the person with whom you have that relationship, the date you spoke on the phone or spent time together, and whether you gave in to his or her wishes or your wants and preferences were given due consideration.

At first you may not even recognize what actually happens in any given situation because you are more comfortable avoiding an argument. You might convince yourself that you really do want to go to a movie instead of out to dinner, or that you would prefer to drive instead of your friend.

Check each individual exchange to see if the truth is that you are subjugating your own choice to find solutions acceptable to everybody. Stay alert and do an honest assessment of the dynamics of your relationships – with friends, family, and co-workers – and write down what happens.

Solution #3: Choose a friend and ask for some help

If after doing the evaluation for Solution #2, you find that it is difficult for you to say no, or that friends may take advantage of you, or that you do tend to care more about the welfare of others than your own, do not allow this awareness to put you in a funk. The other side of this behavioral pattern is that you are a great friend, have qualities that make you easy to get along with, and are very tactful and supportive.

Do not be reluctant to choose a friend with whom you can discuss your evaluations and what you discovered. This will not be a burden to a good friend. Ask her to indulge in a role reversal. This exercise will serve as training. Ask her to spend some time with you and to focus on pleasing you, doing what you want to do, and forcing you to communicate about your wishes. If she is a good friend, she will be happy to help. If not, you will certainly find out about the value of this particular relationship. Then, work hard to feel the feelings that come from allowing others to please you and from putting your needs and desires first.

Solution #4: Kickboxing, karate, or self-defense

Do these sound extreme? We suggest some kind of assertiveness training. These solutions may not be to your liking; however, you might consult your nearby college or park district programs and find courses that promote more assertive behavior. This type of training may assist you with family, friends, at your place of worship, or with relationships at your children's school.

A course that aids in enhancing assertiveness may be even more helpful at work. You know how disconcerting it is when there is a lack of support from managers and coworkers, when there is a highly competitive situation, or when surroundings or circumstances are disorganized and disorderly. We are not suggesting you go out and sock someone in the face. Taking such a course may alter your viewpoints and give you greater comfort in considering your needs and desires on an equal plane with others.

Solution #5: Pick out some relationships and have some fun

Once you've gained insight about how your relationships work, and you worked on getting more for yourself from those relationships, it is a good time to strengthen some of the relationships you truly value.

Types of relationships may span a wide range. Some of them involve your inner core. These are the ones in which you discuss your deepest feelings and share mutual values. Other relationships are more casual. These might involve parents of your children's classmates, church or synagogue friends, or women you know from the neighborhood. The next category may include women you know from the gym, or those you went to school with but don't necessarily stay in close touch, etc. Choose a few of these (this will work with family as well), and plan one of the following to share, perhaps with one relationship from each category:

• Take a trip to the museum

• Go to a bookstore and choose a book for the other person

• Visit a store that has fragrances or soaps, and then have coffee at a café

• Decide to buy gift certificates for one another and have lunch to exchange them

• Go to a photographer and have pictures taken together

• Arrange a trip to the Spa

• Or make up one of these types of activities between you

Martha

Solution #1: Ask the right question

Since you love being right, have high standards, and enjoy logical, systematic approaches, you may consistently run into walls trying to maintain relationships. This is important: it is not always necessary to have a lot of friends. It is vital to have some good friends and to have pleasant, functional relationships with family, fellow workers, and others. There is a meaningful question you will want to ask and answer for yourself: "Am I willing to relax my standards and overlook not so significant but less than perfect things that others do, for the sake of keeping friendships and working relationships?"

Solution #2: Evaluate the Consequences

Give some serious thought to that last question. Think back to many of the challenges you have faced with situations in which you were willing to sacrifice a relationship or greatly threaten it. You were doing this because you were placing your standards higher than the value of that relationship. Your standards are important to you, and rightly so. However, if they are used simply to be right or to enable you to be comfortable with your point of view, you may be exchanging some valuable, beneficial relationships.

Giving in and working to change what seems natural to you is very difficult. However, if you save a good friendship, stop a destructive rift within your family, or preserve a decent relationship with a co-worker, not only will you enjoy the continuation of that relationship, but you'll also feel good about stretching yourself and being disciplined about your choices.

Solution #3: Practice your social skills

You know that when you are busy and hassled, you have a tendency to withdraw and be stubborn. Resist that urge. Instead, make a point to put yourself out there. Where is "out there"? At work, find the group at the lunch table being a little boisterous, and go over and join then. When you see some co-workers involved in a discussion, walk over to them and take part. This applies in playgroups with moms and tots, or with family get-togethers as well. No groups to join? Then by all means, pick up the Park District catalog, go online, consult your church or temple newsletter, and get involved. Join some group that attracts you such as a sports, music, gardening, theatre or social club.

Solution #4: Tips for solidifying or making friendships

You are not comfortable having to socialize. However, once you find a social situation where you are able to enjoy yourself, you do find that you are glad to have gone. So here are some ideas to help you find more situations where you do enjoy a social time.

• Sometimes because of your tendency to want everything perfect and your extremely high standards, you are very tough on yourself. In order to make friends and to be a good friend, it is important to like yourself. Review the section on self-esteem in Chapter One, and realize that no one will ever be perfect. Concentrate on the qualities you have that you like so well about yourself, and then relax and be a friend to yourself.

• Since you require some time to be analytical, to weigh the pro's and con's, and to do things properly, and are so put off by a lack of time to process information or to evaluate consequences and emotionally charged situations, you may find it very difficult to resist judging others who behave quite differently than you think they should. Being judgmental is a kiss of death to relationships.

Remember the adage about walking in another person's shoes. Concentrate on appreciating differences and letting others be who they are, as long as they are kind, fun, and interesting.

• You know how much you dislike being criticized. To make new friends or to keep old ones, it is most helpful to avoid being critical. Instead, look for opportunities to say something nice when you can. Observe, and be quick to complement when it is appropriate and sincere.

• It is really not in your nature to want to take risks. However, if you break some risks down to smaller components, perhaps you will be willing to push yourself. If someone has not called you back, take a risk and call again. If you were not invited with a group of friends, call and ask if you can come along. Often women do not intend to offend; they are busy and preoccupied and sometimes forgetful. If you would like to go to a movie, or would like to have a shopping companion, or want someone to talk to, take the small risk and invite someone to do that with you. You'll find it is quite worth the risk.

• Take the time to listen and to communicate. Relationships always are enhanced when one of the people involved make a point to explain that she knows what the other person means. Thorough communication is important to you. Therefore, you will shine at this and be comforting and helpful to your friends in this way.

Solution #5: Restoration

Because of your ability to figure out how to avoid mistakes, or your intense requirement for quality, you probably often please friends, bosses, parents, and colleagues. However, you can at times be self-righteous or intimidating in your expectation of high quality, or you've been so hard on yourself as a result of near burnout. Because of this, it is very possible that you could have annoyed or angered someone else, causing your relationship with that person to be operating at a level of discomfort. If so, here are some possible actions to restore that relationship(s) to a more comfortable place:

• Send a card. You can apologize and explain in the card or simply say you were thinking of that person and would like to get together.

• Invite that person to lunch.

• Do a favor. If that person has kids, offer to stay with the kids when mom goes out. If your co-worker has a chore to do at lunch, offer to do it when you do your own chore. If you're walking your dog, offer to walk hers. If that person likes opinions when she is buying a new out fit, offer to go along and help. You get the idea.

• Bake some cookies and send them. Buy a plant and send it. Knit something small and useful. Yes, a thoughtful, sweet gift is nice. However, something you make yourself would be even nicer.

• Find the occasional time when you can settle in and make a long phone call to really talk with that person, and listen to everything going on in her life right now.

Be creative...think about that person and just do something she would like; something special just from you.

~five~
Relationships
Sex, Romance & Love

The sweetest joy, the wildest woe is love.
– Pearl Bailey

From one extreme to the other...joy and woe. Most women have undoubtedly experienced both of those emotions in relation to love. Love. It's a subject about which innumerable songs have been written and poems composed, and the cause of innumerable heartbreaks. Love and romance are so subjective. Put 100 women in a room - and we would probably get at least as many definitions and explanations.

Many messages about love have been sent and blatantly given to women, ever since childhood, about what we should want and how to get it. Then there's that famous line, "Women: you can't live with them and you can't live without them," and various combinations of similar sentiments. We believe that line can be reversed, as many of today's modern women feel exactly the same about men!

Joy/woe...we love men/we hate men...love is worth it/no it's not. There are, indeed, a lot of mixed feelings about a very broad subject.

"Romance." Now there's a sweet sounding word. What a comforting concept. On the other hand, if Love is complicated, throw in the closely related subject of Sex – and complicated becomes an understatement.

As broad and complex as this chapter's subject is, there are areas of these three emotion-producing concepts that we can examine in our lives. The

Relationships: Sex, Romance and Love

good news is, adjustments can be made that render these experiences easier and more rewarding.

First, it's true that we begin building our understanding and interpretation of love and romance from our own backgrounds, i.e., how our parents treated one another, our own views of our attractiveness or lack of it, how the subjects of love and sex were introduced to us, and how accepted or rejected we were as pre-teens and teens. Then the brew gets even murkier. The overload of fairy tale princes riding toward us on white horses. The enviable white picket fence with the statistical two-and-a-half children. The myriad ads and communications from books, movies, and TV about our "perfect Holly-Homemaker versus Whore-Madonna" complex. By this time we are lucky if we can maintain our equilibrium, let alone have a healthy and clear reality of what we are to do, not to mention what we want in a man and from a relationship.

Once we get past the myths, we are faced with deciding how we are going to live our lives and where love and sex fit into it. Of course, if we inherently are more comfortable with remaining single or not choosing a heterosexual relationship, often we must deal with being ostracized. With sex alone, we struggle with societal expectations and being honest with ourselves. Then, we meet challenges with making relationships work, communicating with partners, making marriage choices, maintaining self-worth, pleasing others, handling infidelity, and dealing with adjustments.

Much has been made recently about the biological differences between men and women. Lately, these differences are being credited with having a strong influence on people's ability to like and get along with the opposite sex. The impact? There's now yet another factor upon which the success of a relationship can hinge. For us as women, we have traditionally been expected to grow up, learn a trade or make a career, be attractive, have friends, excel at being a good homemaker and great in bed, have a hobby, volunteer, be a multi-tasking mom, and be happy. Now, in addition, we have to learn the new lessons of how our man is like other men, how we are like other women, and how to mold ourselves somehow successfully within this amalgam.

In addition, we are at times confronted with problems of personality dis-

59

orders, alcoholism, mental or physical abuse, drugs, and infidelity from or toward our spouses. The subjects of sex, romance and love are very broad, and we do not attempt to address all problems in this book. We do, however, hope to look at some challenges, and believe you'll find some workable solutions that speak to your particular behavioral style. Together we'll explore our own viewpoints about these subjects, strategies for improving relationships, how to separate some myths from our own realities, some troublesome mindsets, pleasing ourselves and our mates, some roadblocks to romance, and getting comfortable with love and sex.

Solutions to sex, love, and romance:

Hillary

Solution #1: If she jumped off a bridge, would you?

Remember as teenagers when our parents voiced objections to a certain party we were planning to attend or to the clothes we were wearing, and we reasoned with them by saying "All our friends are going to that party!" or "All the kids are wearing them too!" Our parents would often respond with something about the false logic of choosing a course of action just because someone else was doing it.

You are a person who moves fast, makes quick decisions and seeks results, and you often have a lot of success with this pattern. It's not uncommon, however, for you to staunchly believe that your partner should see things from your point of view. We believe you do not want to use the teenage style of reasoning, and you would really not want a mate who thinks exactly as you do.

First of all, you both are basically different in your cultural background, parental upbringing, personalities, likes, dislikes, etc. That's perfectly normal. Decide to stop buying into the myth that each partner must see things as the other one does. You (though you may not be 100% sure of this) are not perfect. Focus on what you like about your mate, and realize that you are better off blending two points of view and not forcing your mate to think as you do. Use your differences to enhance your relationship rather than cause anger and righteousness. You can actually learn to appreciate, joke about, and enjoy differing opinions that expand your viewpoint. Remember to treat your partner with the same respect and appreciation that you would like from your best friend.

Solution #2: Perfection or Bust

Since you have a high level of confidence, can be forceful, and quite competitive, as a single person you may set boundaries by categorizing what is and is not acceptable for a date. The result? You may remain single longer than you would like, or, if you are already married or in a relationship, you may be experiencing problems caused by this kind of thinking.

If you have written a list of "must be's" and "must have's" for your prospective dates, you may have developed a closer relationship with your TV, girlfriends, or pet than you have with a possible life partner. You may have noticed that there is a shortage of ideal, dreamboat spouses. You will wear out your dream machine before you find that perfect image. By insisting that your prospective partner have a certain face, body, age, job, income, etc., you are truly blocking the opportunity to find a loving, supportive, and successful relationship. Start off by being open to possibilities; stop being restrictive. Decide that if you meet someone who seems nice or pleasant, you will go out, have fun, and get to know that person. If you keep your high standards out of the equation, and just let events and experiences unfold, you may discover yourself caring for the person, and not his "stats." By the same token, if you got yourself into a relationship that isn't working because you insisted on certain unrealistic constructs, it is time for you to rethink your choices.

Solution #3: Slow down and lighten up

Since you most often keep yourself extremely busy, and it is important for you to be in control, it is quite possible that these issues manifest themselves in your sex life. For one thing, if you keep so busy that the only time you stop is when you pass out from exhaustion, you might be robbing yourself of full, pleasurable sexual experiences. On the other hand, if control is important to you, you may use it as a tool in negotiations or to win the upper hand with your mate. Either of these types of behaviors can seriously deflect from a happy, healthy sexual relationship.

If you and your mate are only rarely having sex, it's time to have a serious discussion about recommitment. That doesn't mean a casual conversation five minutes before getting into bed. That means finding time alone together and maybe taking time away from home, perhaps a weekend getaway without interruptions such as kids or friends. Set your problems, goals, chores, and worries aside. Do it. Talk and figure out what is necessary to restore your relationship.

If you are using sex to control favors or behaviors, or to settle arguments, you are going to destroy the possibility of a fulfilling, happy relationship. Again, go away with your spouse, and brainstorm other acceptable ways to settle differences, to get attention, to feel loved and respected. If these solutions do not produce results, then it is time to consult a counselor.

Solution #4: Develop the habit

Know how a habit starts and then gets reinforced? By doing something enough times, anything becomes a habit. Examples are smoking, going to and from work using the same route, or eating at the same restaurant on a certain night of the week. You are quite driven to achieve, and this sometimes blocks out the softer, slower, and often warmer aspects to life.

Therefore, it is also true that to bring love and loving feelings into one's life, the best way is by giving love – and giving a lot of it. Do it. Not from the motive to gain, but instead for the sake of loving. You'll see. Love is catching. When you come just from the thought of giving lovingly and giving of yourself in a loving way, you will simply draw love back to you. Sometimes we can spend years looking for love and it escapes us. Once we volunteer in a loving way, take the time to make and give a gift, help someone in need, it is amazing the loving reward we get in return.

Solution #5: Strength training for your heart

With your behavior style, you are often not comfortable with what you may interpret as being soft or weak. Sometimes being romantic, and loving another person by doing loving things, may feel soft or weak to you. Using this outlook, you may want to switch gears and reinvigorate your relationship. In order to do so, you must approach your relationship as a project in the same way you typically handle other things in your life.

Make a list with your significant other of ways you both can wallow in love, and then follow through on doing the things on your list. You may find this practice akin to forcing yourself to keep meditating until you get the hang of it. Some of it may feel silly to you. However, keep at it until you are thoroughly relaxed and having fun. No doubt you'll discover that once you set your mind to this, you and your mate will become creative.

To get you started, some items on your list might be: take care of something your mate wants you to do for him/her; exchange the top five things you like about one another; go shopping together to buy one another sleeping wear, and then go home and try it on; find your favorite passage or quotation and have your mate really listen as you read it aloud, etc., etc. Come on – force yourself! Just as with physical exercise, it takes some time to see the results.

Ivana

Solution #1: Smoke signals make the air murky

To express and communicate is key to a successful relationship. One of our favorite quotes is, "Choose your words for clarity. Don't expect your listeners to do the editing for you." In other words, to get what you want, to relieve discomfort, and to convey your feelings or thoughts, you must use the right code to deliver your message.

You may recognize a tendency in yourself, when under pressure, to exaggerate or oversell your point of view. Therefore, when having a heart-to-heart with your significant other, do something to help calm yourself down before you begin the conversation. That will help increase your control in choosing how to express what you are trying to get across.

You often react impulsively – another aspect of your personality that can lead you to undesirable consequences. When communicating with your partner, the best way to be persuasive is to be specific when trying to get your point across. Use examples about what happened or where you were when a problem arose. Using broad generalizations can spur misunderstandings and injured feelings. Since you can seem manipulative when your intention is to persuade or influence, be certain to keep your voice moderate, steer clear of intense words such as "always," "never," or "every time." Also, stay away from hurtful words, name-calling, insults, and ultimatums.

Solution #2: Use the start-over strategy

You are most likely aware that with your behavioral style, it may not be unusual for you to lack patience with someone who needs time to think and act. Therefore, you may fuel divisions and conflict in your relationships. This can occur whether you are dating or in a long-term relationship. Your mate may not be as spontaneous as you are, or make decisions – as you often do – emotionally or with your gut. If your partner makes decisions more slowly or is considerably more analytical, this may create discord in your relationship.

When these conflicts occur, you may feel you want to get away, flee from the discomfort. A real lack of communication results and your relationship takes on an irreversible, stuck-in-the mud, " there's no way out of this" feeling.

A good way to resolve this dilemma is to count on the sage "be in the present" philosophy. Just start over. That means giving up your need to be right at this moment. It means not holding onto anger, frustration, regrets and disappointments from the past or your intentions for the future. Just as children can suspend their disbelief and instantly become astronauts in a spaceship, dressed-up mommies and daddies at work, or singers in a musical production, you can give up your need to change something at the moment, and put yourself in a state of love. Simply make an agreement with your mate to be loving at this moment. Recall all the traits that created your loving feelings in the first place, and then just start over. This action will kindle a reconnection and remind you both of the preciousness of what you have together.

Solution #3: Making it last

Since your personality in large part dictates your spending so much time in social situations and making a favorable impression, you may find yourself searching for an intimate, bonded relationship. Because of your high energy level around others and your outgoing style, you may find many people to date, and still lack the meaningful and lasting relationship that you seek. Here are some solid strategies to point you toward a successful relationship. Use these approaches, and you will be more likely to reach your relationship goal.

• From your first encounter, focus on communicating the treatment you want and deserve. Make sure you fully express the behavior you expect from this person. Be careful about showing a need to have him define you. If you give him the power to make you feel you are terrific and wonderful, you also give him the power to make you feel bad about yourself. Don't allow your need for acceptance to give him control over how you feel about who you are.

• Delay the urge to have sex early on. This is another good principle to follow to give your relationship a more solid base, and it will give both of you time to get to know the other person.

• Avoid putting more into your relationship than you get out of it. Be cognizant of the amount of time, energy, feelings, and devotion you care to expend in your relationship, and then make certain you get the same in return.

• Have clarity about what your expectations are, and what you will do if those expectations are not met. This is a behavior that should be present from the outset of a relationship. Especially, set your standards for honesty and openness early on in your interactions. If you do not get the same level of exposure then draw back and protect yourself.

• Finally, when seeking a meaningful partnership, always be yourself rather than trying to impress or to be what another person seems to want you to be.

Solution #4: Sexual self-discovery

You may already be aware that, with your behavioral type, getting recognition and receiving praise has a pretty strong influence on your decisions and responses. Just as early learning and experiences can influence our social behavior, this characteristic may affect our adult sexuality. Take two important first steps too learn more about what you want in a sexual relationship. First, take a short break from your sexual relationship with the intention of exploring some facts about it in order to return to the relationship with a deeper love. Secondly, during this break, ask yourself some important questions about what you learned in the past, the beliefs you formed, and how you may want to change some attitudes as well as behaviors.

Use the following questions to assist you in this process:

- How was the subject of sex addressed in my home as I grew up? Was physical affection present with my parents?

- Was I taught to act seductively, but also that sex was to be avoided and something only for "bad" girls?

- Are there any "double standard" messages still affecting my behavior?

- What gives me sexual pleasure?

- Does guilt or psychological manipulation have a role in my sexual attitudes and behavior?

- How powerful do I feel within my sexual relationship compared to other aspects of my relationship?

- How important is sex and intimacy in my life?

- Does my body image cause self-consciousness in bed?

- Do I have complaints about my mate's performance?

- Do I feel my needs are being met?

The answers to these questions – and others that come to mind as a result of this process – will help you develop a stronger sense of your sexuality and establish a healthier sex life. You will be better able to be authentic, rather than reacting in order to get approval. If this exercise does not create greater clarity for you, consider talking with a friend, clergyperson, or doctor.

Solution #5: Zip it

If you take a stark look at yourself and your behavior in the past, you may recognize that being too open about private matters can negatively impact a healthy relationship. In regard to your partner, it's one thing to be open, honest, and want to have a right to vent about dissatisfaction. It's a completely undesirable choice to rant and rave about your significant other, or to make too many personal reports when talking with others about your relationship.

Instead of just getting out of control in order to feel better for a short time, remind yourself that everything you are thinking does not have to be said. Haven't you made that choice in the past, only to regret it and want to take back your words? It's true that expressing your feelings may be helpful. However, some things are just not right to say to anyone. Think before you speak, and consider if what you want to say is in that category.

In regard to sharing the state of your relationship with others, it's been fashionable for people to "let it all hang out" and to say whatever is on their mind. However, that choice can wreak havoc. Instead of letting others know the difficulties and happenings in your relationship, stop and think before shooting off your mouth. Make sure you don't go overboard and begin to seem worse than the person you're complaining about.

There are alternatives to saying whatever you feel like saying. Here are some possibilities:

• Imagine saying whatever you feel like saying, just to get rid of the discomfort of holding it in. Then take a deep breath and re-think how much and what you want to say.

• Go for a run, hit a pillow, or throw a ball as hard or fast as you can… find some way to exert enough energy that the urge to blast forth passes.

• Watch a TV show, read a book, journal, or go to the movies. Choose something that can divert the anger of the moment and get some space between the urge to explode your message and the comfort of knowing there's a better way.

Laura

Solution #1: Get out the wine, the gourmet meal, the soft music, and dance…

When confronted with frustration or heavy challenges, your two common modes of behavior may be to withdraw or react negatively to change. So, if you have been looking a long time for a romantic relationship or are currently in a relationship lacking in romance, there are things you can do to rectify the situation.

- Check out your attitude about romance. Go back into your past and remember what was the most romantic time of your life. If that doesn't work, recall the most romantic moment from a fantasy or dream. Let what you discover be a guide as you consider your behavior and that of your suitor or significant other.

- If you are single and searching for love, consider if you are hampering your chances by doing any of the following:

    –Harboring unrealistic expectations of men

    –Avoiding social situations because of the fear of rejection

    –Thinking only of what you'll get out of a relationship instead of what you can give as well.

    –Setting yourself up to be completely different from everyone else, thereby concluding you'll never find someone for you.

    –Being either too promiscuous or too offended by a sexual overture.

    –Setting up an ideal that no person can meet or live up to.

    –Passing on opportunities to go to places where you can meet a possible suitor.

    –Holding off on being happy, productive, active now, in the belief that once you have a loving relationship, everything will be perfect.

    –Going out only with gay or married men

    –Feeling that if you have a demanding career, there is no room for love.

- Romance requires some nurturing. So practice being sensitive to "reading" messages sent to you by someone you might be interested in or by your partner. It's difficult to know how to do this. However, when a baby or small child is ill, he or she cannot often tell us exactly what is wrong. We kind of "read" the signals. This procedure is very similar.

- Be willing to be a little courageous in your response. This doesn't mean drastic change. It requires, again, some sensitivity. Perhaps something as bold as sending a man flowers or simply overloading on compliments when you can legitimately find those opportunities, picking up a book or renting a movie you think he'd particularly love more than you would, and then there's always that foot massage.

• Avoid doing the same thing you usually do when in one another's company or going on a "date." Instead, engage in an actual activity as opposed to the movie and dinner. Bowl, go to an amusement park, play a sport together, play a board game, etc. This tends to lessen tension, helps conversation flow, and creates a great atmosphere for getting to know one another either better or in a different light.

Solution #2: All you need is love, sweet love

Not actually...simply loving someone else does not solve all problems. In your case, security is such a big motivating force that you may be willing to sacrifice your own needs by putting them last in your relationship.

It's not always easy to identify your needs or to put them into words. Sometimes, you may even avoid expressing your needs to avoid conflict. Although it may be a scary thing to do, it is necessary to find out your needs and then express them to your partner. Failure to do so results in feeling unhappy, feeling frustrated and distant from someone you love, and not truly living your life. So take the risk and examine your needs. To make it easier, think of the types of needs you have as spiritual, physical, emotional, social or practical. Write down these types of needs as column headings, and then use a stream of consciousness approach to listing needs under each. Write down whatever comes to mind.

• Spiritual needs may mean respect for your religious choices, respect for your beliefs, the need to go to a place of worship when and where you want.

• Physical needs include being comforted and caressed, or kissing, hugging, and sex.

• Emotional needs might include the need to feel deeply about a person, a book or movie; to get recognition for some accomplishments, to not always be perfect or act "right"; to feel desired; to be special to your lover; to hear how your partner feels about you, etc.

• Social needs can involve hand-holding in social situations, being included in your partner's social plans, being treated politely, having attention in social situations, having support when with others, etc.

- Practical needs could include not being threatened when there is conflict; knowing your partner will be there when you are vulnerable; knowing you have a say-so in important decisions; knowing your partner will be true to you; knowing you can rely on your partner for comfort, etc.

Once you know what you need, you must express these needs. Then, perhaps most importantly, monitor your daily life to make sure you are doing whatever is necessary to have your needs met.

Solution #3: Is Meryl Streep in the house?

In a relationship, there are a great many components that contribute to its success, such as common likes and dislikes, doing things for your partner to show how much you care, overlooking minor irritations, etc. One important aspect of a relationship that often gets overlooked is the role we take on in the relationship and the disharmony it can sometimes cause. What often happens is that we get set in our ways. It's as if we have been cast in a play or movie and feel compelled to play a role. Most often we are not aware we are doing this.

As a result, we tend to blame our partners for what is happening when actually our own behavior is equally responsible. Two traits consistent with your personality are patience and persistence. These are admirable characteristics, and they are valuable in relationships – unless you go too far and play the role of the agreeable woman willing to withstand anything and everything. It's important to examine the role you are playing and consider whether some situations improve as a result.

For instance, you may blame your partner for always finding fault with you. But then, instead of expressing your feelings, you choose to quietly and continually feel resentful. Stop playing that "poor–me" role. Make the decision to cast aside the victim role, and in a strong yet loving way, let your partner know how you feel. Take responsibility for allowing your partner's behavior to irritate you.

Or, since you are so patient, you may stew each and every time your partner is late. Yet, you do nothing but wish he were different. This behavior builds distance between you. Instead, during a quiet time when you both are in a more relaxed mood, address this habit and explain how that makes you feel. Say something like, "I feel irritated when you are late. I would prefer it if you either tell me you'd be here at a later time, or make it a point to be on time." Then you can both work on a plan to avoid this consistent tardiness. That way you will be accepting your responsibility in the outcome.

Decide to look for ways in which you stay stuck in a habitual role or persistent patterns of reacting. Once you have done that, you can work with your partner to develop alternate ways to behave.

Solution #4 Self-diagnose and order the right prescription

You are a very patient person and are often motivated by acceptance. But your eagerness to be accepted and your willingness to be patient and trusting may be creating relationship problems in your life. You may be involved with someone who is married, or staying in a relationship too long without getting commitment, or trusting your friend too easily. Each of these could result in your being hurt. If this describes you, it's time to begin an examination of your relationship. Get out your prescription pad.

Are you involved with someone who continues to lead you on and never get beyond his promises? Does the person you meet promise to call you, and then the phone doesn't ring? Do your inclinations to be friendly, accepting, and trusting leave you frustrated and disappointed with potential partners? If so, you must acknowledge this trend in your life. Once you face the relationship illness that persists in your life, you can discover the right treatment.

Here are some suggestions to establish healthier relationships:

• Decide in advance what and whom you want to avoid. Using your past experience, actually write down the types of behavior and actions that are no longer acceptable to you. If you have trouble doing this, read books or listen to tapes on these subjects, or consult with a coach or counselor.

• Decide on what and whom you want. Without being too rigid, write down some of the characteristics you are looking for in a relationship. Then when you meet someone new, in your private time consult your list. If that person doesn't have the traits that are necessary for you to be happy and healthy, cut that person loose immediately. No ifs, ands, buts, excuses, delays or willingness to see what happens. Do it now! Drop that person right now!

- Get yourself involved in situations where you can meet new people. We know, easier said than done. A few standard suggestions that you may have already considered are classified ads, computer matchmaking sites, adult-education courses (choose subjects that genuinely interest you), volunteer and hobbyist organizations, bookstores and coffee shops, etc. Also advise family and friends that you would like to meet someone new.

Solution #5: Take a good look in the bedroom

As you know, you may be too willing to put up with certain uncomfortable situations. You also care a great deal about close relationships. These are two good reasons to see if the sexual side of your relationship is working best for you and your lover. As you may have discovered already in this book, attitudes and beliefs play such an important part in how our lives are working. See if any of these beliefs may be creating intimacy problems for you.

- We've been together so long that, after awhile, expecting fireworks in the bedroom is unrealistic.

- We are so busy that once we get – (fill in the blank; a vacation, past this financial setback, the kids off to college, through this project he has at work) – we'll have more time for each other.

- I've put on so much weight that I don't feel attractive.

- I can't expect my sex life to be like the movies or the romance novels I read.

- We are so affectionate and nice to one another that sex really isn't important.

- There are too many problems in our lives to worry about sex.

- I never have an orgasm/he doesn't care to make me happy so it's not worth it anyway.

If you can relate to any of the above statements, you need to recognize

their consequences on your relationship and your life. Take steps to do something about it. These are false beliefs that do not have to persist. This time you absolutely must consult a doctor or counselor, and make some necessary changes.

Martha

Solution #1: The big "C" or making sure to get it right

You realize that criticism has a big influence in your life. You are very uncomfortable when others criticize what you do, because doing everything right is so important to you. Also, since you have such high standards and take great care in all that you do, you feel justified in expecting others to do the same. You may harshly judge what others do and the way they do it. This attachment to criticism may often affect your relationship with your mate. You know, the old, familiar toilet seat and toothbrush squeezing styles, the "my partner does it one way and I do it the other way" conflicts. It is so easy to lose touch with what is really important within a relationship and in life. When you have made painstaking attempts to have things a certain way, and along comes your partner and forgets or ignores instructions on how things are done, you may be prey to an emotional outburst.

Instead, since you love organization, take a seat and write down what can be categorized as "Minor Irritations" or "Irksome Violations." In another column, perhaps entitled "What Really Counts," write down what in your mind is of great life importance that rightfully would cause anyone, anywhere to strongly react. Examples for the "Irksome" column might be, "puts the wrong clothes in the dryer," "doesn't put the cap back on a jar in the fridge," etc. The other column might include, "infidelity," "lying," etc. After you complete the lists, decide that you are going to be patient, kind, and light-hearted about the times your partner commits the acts in column one. This will ensure a smoother, happier environment for both participants in your relationship.

As for your discomfort with criticism, make a pact with your significant other that you get the same treatment. Decide together that the small irritations he may have with you are dealt with in the same way you are now handling them. Putting this practice into action may rely on the willingness of both of you to change a few habits. However, you will find the result well worth it.

Solution #2: Ease off, Dr. Freud

You have had much success in life being analytical, cautiously examining options, and taking what some may consider a cool or calculating approach to most matters. This style could hamper your desire for a romantic or lasting relationship. Because you may be overly analytical or too much the perfectionist in your search for the right person, following are some of the pitfalls you definitely want to avoid:

• **Pitfall: Setting unreachable standards.** Looking for the proverbial prince on a white horse? In your case he may not have to be the handsome, dashing hero to come rescue you. However, you might have set certain unmovable standards that create an obstacle to finding love. Get out that checklist you made, whether in your head or on paper, and start scratching things out. If you insist that your mate be a certain age, have a certain job, like certain hobbies, you might as well go out and get some fabric, stuffing, dye or paint, and black buttons for eyes – because you're going to have to construct him out of those materials and sleep with that every night. Go out and get to know someone who seems likeable enough. Forget those rigid standards, and just see what happens.

• **Pitfall: Waiting until he changes.** So you found someone you like well enough, but dang those habits that bug you. Now you find yourself thinking, "he's a nice person but this person could dress better, get a better job, be more socially adept," and on and on. Better hang on to the Construct Fabric Guy described above because you'll spend an eternity trying to change the one you found.

• **Pitfall: Thinking, "Can't have career and love, too."** You have certainly done a great job planning your life, making sure that you have accomplished what you deemed right to accomplish, and you are pretty darn successful. Don't punish yourself by buying into that false idea that once a woman spends a good portion of her life working on schooling and career goals, she's passed the chance to have a good relationship. Bunk! You certainly, in this case, can have your cake (career) and eat it too (love)!

- **Pitfall: If there's no chemistry, don't pursue it.** Being analytical is certainly close to logical. Logically speaking, you reason, "If I am to wind up with the "correct" person, the chemistry must be right." Wrong! So many relationships have grown into loving, lasting, successful relationships because people have had the good sense to appreciate other good characteristics about the person or the relationship. The chemistry can develop and a loving connection happen after liking the person, after enjoying his/her company, after appreciating how he/she treated you.

- **Pitfall: The other person involved in a relationship with you never gets to know or appreciate you.** Often you take the indirect approach, you examine details to size-up someone, and you consider all there is to consider so that you make the right choices. You are so involved with figuring out how he/she is, how he/she acts, seeing if he/she lives up to your expectations, that you are never just being – and so that other person may be out with an attractive calculating machine. Remember, you are a human being and he/she too must find out who and what kind of person you are. So tear up that Standards List on occasion, and go out and have a good time.

Solution #3: Whose sexual morés?

Since correctness and high standards for yourself and others are so important to you, you may have had some conflicts in your sex life. There have been rules that women in our culture have been expected to follow. Yet, those rules went against what may have been natural, pleasant, and good for women.

- While growing up, women often got the message that sex was dirty and that we were bad if we had sex before we were married. True, that standard has relaxed a bit. However, the taint of it may remain in us psychologically. So take a look at your sexual behavior and see if that "rule" influenced you. If there is a remnant of that viewpoint operating today for you, take steps to recognize its origin, and then make sure you work to let it go.

- Another ancient message: it's okay for women to have sexual pleasure as long as the man is satisfied. If not, the rule or tradition is that we are not good "whores" as all women must be for their husbands. So if you have any guilt or feel less self-esteem because you enjoy sex when your mate hasn't been completely satisfied, or because doing so makes you somehow less attractive or less than a good partner in bed, get rid of those ridiculous thoughts and recognize them as false lessons.

• Another strong societal dogma was that orgasm should be reached only through sexual intercourse. We now know, of course, that this is not so. However, you may still be influenced into thinking that it's the only right way to have an orgasm. Sexual pleasure achieved through clitoral stimulation is a woman's choice. Examine your attitude about this aspect of sex to make sure that your proclivity for rightness doesn't deprive you of your own sexual expression.

• Early on, women were influenced to be restrictive in their sexual desire. Recently in our history, however, messages to be sexually free are rampant. Our movies, songs, and advertising messages have clobbered us with attitudes that we almost have a duty to fulfill our sexual desires – to the point of having multiple partners and throwing away any and all restrictions. Of course, this is nonsense. We still have a responsibility to ourselves to conduct ourselves according to what would be safe and sensible for our own lives. So, if the current sway tells us that if we are to be the modern woman and make our sexual satisfaction a ruling factor, your inclination to do the right thing may create an inverted confusion for you. Just be aware of this ill-formed dictate, know what's right for you, and behave accordingly.

• Some other cultural messages cause confusion and dysfunction in relationships. For instance, some consider a woman a "good" partner if she responds to her partner's sexual desires. If she doesn't want sex at a particular moment, she is "cold in bed." Or, unless she meets certain standards of what men consider attractive or proper behavior, she doesn't deserve sex. If men reject women, the follow-up conclusion is that the woman is undesirable, rather than the male has the problem. What's important for you to know is that these standards are set by a male construct, and largely picked up and accepted by society. In fact, they are false standards and do not represent reality or what is true for women. You must not let your own sexual behavior result from what you have been led to believe is right by random, ill-conceived societal rules. You must come to know yourself and set your standards for what is right based on your self-knowledge and care for your partner.

Solution #4: Let the "good ole days" go

We realize our parents had certain circumstances in their lives that determined a set of standards. However, being our parents, they had tremendous influence on our thinking processes as we grew. Since these beliefs were drummed into us as well by teachers, by clergy, and by the world that has considerably changed, we may not realize that some of the following mindsets still linger in heterosexual relationships:

• Stand by your man, no matter what.

• Mr. Right and you like the same things and think alike.

• In a relationship, it is your duty to make your mate happy.

• Love is all that matters.

• Accept things as they are and your life will be easier.

• Be quiet and respect your man.

• If you are a good wife, you will take care of your man first.

If any of these concepts reflect rules you still live by – and some of them may have elements of truth for some people, ask yourself if they apply to who you are and what your needs are. Then take some steps to adjust how you act based on your beliefs. If what you are doing is causing some problems in your relationship, make a plan to change what you're doing. If that seems too complex or difficult, seek additional help from a counselor.

Solution #5: Who really wants to eat off the floors?

Perhaps you have heard of the old compliment about the great skills of the wonderful housekeeper: "You could eat off her floor." That was the ultimate compliment for the good wife who keeps her spouse happy with a clean home. With your behavioral style, it may be easier for you to get caught up in the details of what a good relationship may appear to be instead of the true makings of a relationship. You have an inclination to focus on a task rather than the people who are important to you. If you concentrate on having your finances in perfect order, or on decorating your home so that you win the Seal of Approval from Good Housekeeping magazine, or on having the contents of your pantry labeled and alphabetized, you may not have any energy left to devote to yourself to your relationship.

Take some time to look at your relationship. Can you sense a distance existing in your relationship? Does it feel as if you are close with your significant other? Do you seem to be living in the same house, but not sharing your lives? If those questions resonate with you, you may want to have a little mess in your home or let the bills pile up a bit, just so you can pay more attention to the person you love.

~six~

Belief System

If you believe you can, you can.

If you believe you can't, you can't.

The belief system is very powerful. Beliefs can hold us back without our even knowing why we can't succeed on an important project.

We begin developing our beliefs in early childhood when we are strongly influenced by parents, older siblings, and close relatives. Some beliefs are positive and some are negative. As children, we are too young to discern. As we grow older, we begin to experience the beliefs of others. Again, some beliefs are positive and some are negative. Our belief system expands. As young adults we are better able to assess these beliefs to determine which ones we will keep and which ones we'll reject. Beliefs change as we experience life and we mature.

Our view of the world is shaped by these beliefs. Some of our beliefs that are linked to strong values stay with us over our lifetime. We may reshape them, but frequently the core of the belief remains with us. An example: We may reject some of our religious beliefs from our youth, but when we are in a desperate situation, where do we turn first?

When our beliefs are challenged, we have the choice to alter the belief or hold onto it no matter what happens. When our egos are involved in the belief, we plant both feet and refuse to change no matter what. Change is not easy, even when the belief is causing us problems. Some of our beliefs

seem to be hardwired into our innermost being.

Most of you have probably heard the statement: "the apple doesn't fall far from the tree." We learn from our parents and those beliefs can help us succeed or keep us from going past a certain level of success. This is why it's important to be open to suggestions when someone we trust, such as a coach or mentor, recommends that we change because something we are doing is holding us back.

We also have societal beliefs (messages) that become our beliefs. These societal beliefs are sometimes hard to overcome. Women have been working on equality with men for decades. Progress is made very slowly. As a society, we still hold onto the belief that men are somehow superior to women or that one race is superior to another. This can be very subtle, but it remains in our underlying belief system.

Beliefs can become all consuming, such as in the Israeli-Palestinian conflict or the Catholic-Protestant conflict in Ireland. Each side believes the other is completely wrong. These beliefs are so all consuming that people sacrifice themselves. These beliefs have lived for generations. It is extremely difficult to change such cultural beliefs.

This chapter addresses the individual beliefs that are common for someone with your preferred behavioral style. Beliefs are at the core of our being. We all have them. Even when the belief is negated by hardcore evidence, we tend to disbelieve the facts. Beliefs are involved in our decision-making process. If I believe that the glass ceiling at my office cannot be broken, I probably will not apply for the executive level position – the belief may or may not be true, but that is my belief regarding the system. Some of us will challenge the belief while others will tell ourselves "what's the use."

Stephen Covey said, "As long as you think the problem is out there, that very thought is the problem." Those thoughts come from our beliefs. Beliefs generate thoughts that generate emotions that impact our actions. We can cause ourselves a multitude of problems by not challenging, or not even recognizing, some of these beliefs. We all, at times, express an espoused, or perceived, theory in use when in fact we have a different or actual theory in use. It often takes a third party to point that out to us.

Awareness is the first step in overcoming beliefs that are self-defeating. Listen to what you are telling yourself in stressful situations. Listen when others give you feedback on how your beliefs are affecting you. Try not to become defensive and blocked to suggestions, both of which will keep you stuck. Some self-defeating beliefs may be: "I am not good enough to do _____," "I need _____ to be happy" or "I'm too young or too old to _____."

Beliefs I hold that are holding me back:

Self-defeating belief	Problems it is causing me

Hillary

Solution #1: Understand that all success does not require immediate results

Hillary tends to believe that if you do not get results quickly, you are failing or someone else is causing you to fail. You learned at an early age that getting quick results made you successful. Often you're not aware that you are exerting excessive pressure to get results because you are so focused on getting the results quickly.

If you do fail to get results quickly, it will not kill you. You can learn from failure. Too often you tend to believe that you need the results now and you get very impatient. Think of Thomas Edison who failed many times when inventing the light bulb. He was persistent and, each time, learned one more way that didn't work on his road to success.

Patience is not easy for you. To wait to reach your goals is difficult. When you don't get results quickly, look for the lessons learned on your way to reaching that goal.

Hire a coach or ask someone to be your mentor. Become aware of how your need for immediate results is affecting your outcome. If the situation is affecting your family, have your significant other or spouse give you feedback on your behavior. Just promise not to bite their head off when they're giving you feedback on your forcefulness!

Solution #2: Not everyone is as assertive as you are

How many times have you looked at another woman and thought, "what a milquetoast!" Many women have succumbed to the societal belief that they shouldn't be competitive and talk about their many successes. Not you. You will compete with anyone to win. Your belief that passive women are not worth getting to know may keep you from making some excellent friendships. These women may only need a role model. Make yourself available to mentor others.

A big challenge for many women is being too passive and not standing up for themselves. You have no problem with this. Teach other women that beliefs regarding the need to please others are not healthy. Be certain that you yourself have mastered the ability to be assertive and are not aggressive in these situations.

You've probably been able to ascend the corporate ladder because of your beliefs that you are just as qualified, or more qualified, than many male executives. Reach down and bring some women along with you. Be a role model for them. This will help you realize that you are not better than other women but have learned to successfully navigate the system.

Be available to help others understand the importance of meeting their own needs. If they only pay attention to others' needs, they won't be around long to look after themselves or others. This is the oxygen mask rule: put your mask on first, and then assist others.

Solution #3: Start trusting others; at least those who are trustworthy

Others are capable of taking responsibility. If you are a parent or some-one in authority, you may believe others don't measure up to your amaz-ing skills. If you treat others as irresponsible, they will act irresponsibly. When you believe you have control over others and exert that control, you take on the responsibility for them.

Let go of some of your control. You won't disintegrate! It is the paradox of giving up control to gain control. Trust your children or your line staff or friends to have the skills they need to accomplish the tasks. They will feel respected and try to do 110%. If they don't know the process, teach them as a mentor would.

Ivana

Solution #1: Being the center of attention at all the times can be stressful

Your tendency to believe you need social recognition to feel valued may be defective. Get a job or hobby where you can be up front and noticed. Get your social needs met there. When that job or hobby is completed, sit back and listen to others for a while. Intentionally keep your mouth closed and listen.

Count to 10 before you jump in and take over the conversation. Ask others about their likes and dislikes. You'll be amazed at the response you get. People will value you for showing them respect and giving them time to be heard. You will then feel their acceptance.

Solution #2: It is not required that you be in a relationship 100% of the time

Your belief that you can't find security in yourself may be flawed. By developing your self-confidence and getting to know your inner self, you will feel more secure. Even though you may appear very self-confident, many times you have your doubts that you can survive on your own. Ivana sometimes impulsively runs from one person to another just to feel that sense of belonging and acceptance.

You may not be aware of this belief. Check it out. Have relationships caused you problems? When you broke off a relationship, were you quickly looking for another one or feeling lost without one? Have you stayed in an unhealthy relationship just because you were afraid to be on your own? It is okay to need other people, but to be constantly in one relationship or another magnifies your belief that you need someone else for security.

Solution #3: Saying "no" will not necessarily mean you will miss out on all the fun

Set some goals for what, when, where, and how you will get your needs met. When someone asks you to do something or go somewhere, stop and determine whether this will help you accomplish your goals. Practice saying "no" and challenge your belief that you will miss out.

Stephen Covey said, "You have to decide what your highest priorities are and have the courage – pleasantly, smilingly, non-apologetically – to say 'no' to other things. And the way you do that is by having a bigger 'yes' burning inside. The enemy of the 'best' is often the 'good.'"

Laura

Solution #1: The belief that I always have to be accommodating and pleasing is flawed

To please everyone in order to be accepted only puts you in a subservient position that no one respects. One of the first things Laura needs to learn is that it is impossible to please all of the people all of the time. Trying to be accommodating and pleasing all the time only adds to the frustration of not getting your needs met – and it leaves you feeling victimized.

Challenge this belief by intentionally trying not to please people. This will be very hard. Ask for a trusted friend's help to stand up for your own needs. Others may be amazed and somewhat taken back by your behavior change, but they will learn to respect you for standing up for yourself. And if they were using you only for what you could do for them, they weren't your friend in the first place.

Solution #2: Start making requests for what you need

Stop apologizing before you ask a question. Start believing that you are just as valued as any other person. Start making requests that will meet your needs. When a relationship is one-sided, you lose your sense of self-worth; you feel less of a person than the other person.

Changing the belief that others are better than you can be very difficult. You have probably felt this way all your life. When you consciously become aware of how you treat yourself and others, you can start getting rid of this monstrous belief.

Being bold may take some time. Work with a friend or a coach to practice speaking with authority. When changing you may come across as aggressive; you can always tone that down with practice.

Solution #3: I do not need to help and take responsibility for every problem

With the belief that you need to be a caretaker for others, you can spend hours worrying about whether you have done the right thing. You may believe everything is your fault. Problems and chaos can make you uncomfortable. Many women are conditioned to feel responsible for everything. Because of this over-responsibility, you begin to feel blame for everything or begin to blame others for your problems. Worry and guilt only intensify the situation. By accepting the reality that you do not have control over others, you have taken the first step in challenging this belief.

Start recognizing that others also have responsibilities. I don't have to take on the whole world. I am not a bad person if I work on getting my own needs met. When you think about it, you may have spent so many years thinking about others' needs that you haven't a clue as to what you really need. You may want to start journaling or writing down the things that begin to surface when you begin focusing on your needs.

Solution #4: Disagree with others when you don't agree with what they say

Your opinion is just as important as anyone else's opinion. Never disagreeing with others and never expressing your opinions only hurts you. Females have frequently been placed in the role of peacekeeper. The belief that you need to keep the peace may only stifle your initiatives. Conflict cannot all be avoided. It is important to allow some conflict in order to get opinions aired and issues resolved.

Change is usually very difficult for you. Start by being aware of your feelings when there is a disagreement. Remind yourself that there frequently needs to be disagreement before everyone can come to a consensus. If you continue to passively agree, resentments will begin to build. No one wants to be around when you blow! Feelings not expressed will show up in your behaviors, often at inappropriate times. Passive resistance can also keep you from experiencing the benefits of change.

When you start expressing your opinions, whether controversial or not, you can begin to feel you are of value and do have a voice in the situation. Have a friend or mentor help you express yourself in an appropriate manner. Be aware that when you first try to be assertive, you may sometimes come across as aggressive. This is only normal when changing behaviors. Encourage your mentor to help formulate how you want to express your opinion. With practice you, too, can have your opinions heard.

Martha

Solution #1: No one can be right 100% of the time

Women are often told to be careful and not make mistakes. You frequently believe that you need to avoid mistakes at all costs. This can have an adverse effect on you for life. You won't dare to take risks. You will have trouble making decisions. You will want everything perfect. This can cause you to set unrealistic expectations that ultimately lead to failure.

Avoiding mistakes is unrealistic. Leaders now are challenged to work quickly, make snap decisions, and produce results. Perfectionism only saps your energy and bogs down your career advancement. Perfectionism not only causes you to set unrealistic goals for yourself, but also affects the way you treat others. With perfectionism nothing that you do is ever good enough, and nothing others do is good enough either.

Challenge that belief by allowing yourself to be okay with making a mistake or two. It is not the end of the world, and others will not even remember. Let go of this control. Work on progress, not perfection. You may need the help of someone else to overcome this perfectionist belief, since it probably developed in early childhood.

Try starting by intentionally doing things more quickly and ignoring the fact that you made a couple of mistakes. This will be very difficult! Use a trusted friend as a sounding board to help you from getting your self worth tied up in the outcome.

Solution #2: It is impossible to treat everyone equally

Because of your belief that everyone needs to be treated fairly, you may start worrying about whether you are spending as much money on a gift for one person as you did for another. Or you may worry about being fair with your children or everyone at the office. Somehow you feel that if you treat others fairly, they will treat you fairly because it's the right thing to do.

In many business and personal situations, differential treatment has to be considered. If you don't accept differential treatment as an option, you will spend all of your energy and time trying to keep things fair. Each situation needs to be evaluated separately. Differential treatment does not mean unfair. Not everyone wants to be treated in the same way. We each have different needs.

The other result of this fairness principle may be that you feel you are being treated unfairly. Talk to the person you feel is precipitating this belief. Try to keep an open mind about what they say. This will keep you out of the victim role. To just sit and feel victimized is not pleasant for you or others around you. Keep in mind: "The world is not always fair!"

Solution #3: I can break the rules – everything is not black and white

Many women are taught that good girls obey all the rules at all times. "You must act properly. If you abide by all the rules, you will be a success." Do all rules make sense? Do you still pressure yourself into obeying the rules even when they don't make sense? Do you allow yourself any exceptions?

The truth is that most rules had a purpose at one time or another, for some reason, to someone. Start challenging some of the rules that don't make sense. For every rule, there is an exception. Rules frequently need to be changed to fit the situation. Stop blindly following the rules that don't fit with your situation. The best selling leadership book a few years ago was **First Break All the Rules**. Strong adherence to the rules limits opportunity, flexibility, and creativity. Breaking the rules can lead to phenomenal success!

If you believe you can, you can. If you believe you can't, you can't.

~seven~

Finances

Money is tied to our values, as well as our egos.

Disagreements regarding finances have been cited as the top reason why people have problems in relationships. The discussion of money frequently stirs up strong emotions. In addition, we often have "hot buttons" when discussing finances. Whether single or married, we may often fight internally with ourselves or externally with others about the issue of spending money. Many times we either don't want to stay within our budget, or we think we don't deserve any extravagances. We may rationalize and justify why we deserve something expensive. Or at other times we may do the opposite – deny ourselves purchases that we rightfully deserve and could afford.

Most women have grown up with a distorted reality when it comes to money. If we had everything we wanted when growing up, we may still feel entitled to have everything now. If we felt we were deprived during childhood, we either think we deserve better now or, the opposite, we still have the mentality of poverty. The truth is, these feelings are rarely based on the reality of our bank account.

It is only recently that financial experts have begun to educate us on smart ways to handle our money. Many financial consultants have also filled the void, helping us understand how to use our money to attain our life's goals. In the past, family and close friends may have tried to offer helpful advice that proved not very helpful. Though well intentioned, these individuals rarely know more than we do, and they've actually been instrumental in our holding onto the beliefs that have gotten us into trouble.

Years ago a woman was groomed to catch the "right" man who would take care of her. Today some women continue to feel they need a man for financial security. Unfortunately many women have ended up flat broke when their husbands left them. Many were not educated to take care of themselves financially while they took care of their husbands and children. Men frequently got the majority of the money when relationships ended.

Where do we spend our money? If we want to marry, should we marry for love, or for money? Often we want money because it is connected to our self-confidence, or linked to our feelings of success. How much money is enough? The truth is: no amount seems to be enough. The more we make, the more we spend!

Anyone seeking to live life at an optimal level needs to examine her relationship with money. Women have the reputation for not understanding finance and not being able to manage money. While this is mostly a myth, it is still true for many women. And it needs to change for any woman who wants to have an adequate amount of money in the future.

We usually have some trouble attaining, and then maintaining, the lifestyles that we want. Many times we feel we're the only ones having financial problems. We feel financially stuck at a certain level. Also, we may be desperately involved in trying to keep up with the Joneses. Later we find out that the Joneses themselves have a $40,000 BMW and are $38,000 in debt for that car. Is this what we want for ourselves? Clearly our behavior around money is a choice, and one where our own personal style can sometimes cause problems for us.

Solutions for finances:

Hillary

Solution #1: Assess priorities

Usually Hillary works very hard to get the results she needs. Stop and ask yourself: "Is this achievement something that I value, or have I become caught up in getting more money?" The danger here is that the need for control or achievement sometimes takes on a life of its own.

When Hillary becomes driven by things alone, she forgets what she really values. Frequently, she becomes so results oriented that she steps on friends and family on her way to achieve them, all the while not seeming to care about others' needs. Do you value money more than family and friends? It is important to become aware of this tendency. Usually Hillary is not even aware of the degree to which some of her bold moves have a negative impact on others. Check this out – is this happening to you?

Solution #2: Plan for the unknown

The more Hillary can feel in control of her money today, the less fear she will have about not having enough in the future. Continue working on those plans to reach your goals. It's never too early to plan for your future. Examine your insurance needs. Each time you make major changes, such as having a child, moving to a different home, or retiring, meet with your advisor to adjust your policy. Update your will. It's hard to accept the fact that there may be need, but accidents and illnesses do occur.

Solution #3: Budget for your dreams

Hillary is a risk-taker; yet she likes to be in control. She wants to be able to move money quickly if some uncertainty exists. She frequently gets bored and impatient with having her finances in low-risk accounts that don't show strong results.

Determine, along with your financial consultant, what percentage of your money you can invest in high-risk ventures and what percentage you need to keep in the lower risk category. Make a list of your goals so that your finances can meet these goals. Save for the things that you value, such as time with your family, a dream vacation or a condo in the city.

Realizing your Dream

Your Value/Dream	Financial Goal	Results

Ivana

Solution #1: Don't spend more than you have! (a.k.a. Ouch! Those credit card bills!)

Since Ivana wants social recognition, money can become a real battleground in any relationship as well as a huge budgeting problem. When in the midst of impulsively buying something, STOP! Ask yourself, "Is this item something that I need or value, or am I looking to get someone's attention?" Be as honest as possible with the reason that you are spending money. Social prestige can become an all-consuming drive. If you don't care to curb your spending, get a high paying job or marry someone very wealthy!

You may need to have the help of a professional to work on eliminating credit card debt. Try to do some long term planning, and keep in mind that even though planning can be boring, it does work!

Solution #2: Don't let the details of future planning slide

Sometimes in all the activity of everyday life, planning takes last place. Be alert! What are you planning to do with your money? If you don't want to work with the boring details, hire a trustworthy advisor who will handle them for you. Also have an advisor examine your insurance needs and make a will. There is nothing like an unexpected occurrence to knock you flat on your rear end. It is so easy in the good times to let these things slide.

Some financial experts have also advised women to maintain some "secret" accounts that could be accessed in an emergency. That means not telling others about them, because then you may be pressured to disclose or share. Since you have problems not telling everything, do keep a tight lip if you choose to go this route. There are many pros and cons to secretive behaviors. You can look at it as emergency money. Men do it all the time!

Solution #3: Look for a flexible budget

Ivana usually has a terrible time staying within a budget. There is nothing more obnoxious to her than having to stay within certain boundaries and pay attention to the details. But sometimes it can be worth it. Even though it's often hard to stay with goals and follow through with boring plans, in the end you could have your dream. What is important to you?

Usually social recognition has a high priority. You love people and that is where you get your needs met. Complete the "Realizing your Dream" table below. Doesn't it appear to be worth it to budget?

Realizing your Dream

Your Value/Dream	Financial Goal	Results

Laura

Solution #1: Don't give it all away!

Since Laura cares so much about everyone else, she has a tendency to spend money for everyone else's needs and wants, and forget about her own needs and wants. Financial security is important to you. Remember, if you don't take care of your own needs, you could become frustrated and then feel abused. People who give and give eventually feel neglected. If you do spend on your family and friends as well as on yourself, you may run up more debt than you had planned. Others will like you even if you don't give them expensive gifts. And if they stop liking you because you become frugal, they weren't really your friends in the first place.

Solution #2: Plan for the future

Laura has a tendency to focus her thinking more in the here and now than on the future. She may procrastinate and never get around to planning for retirement, examining her insurance needs or making a will. If dealing with these things is not something that you care to do, get the help of a trusted advisor who can tell you what you need to do to have a financially secure future. You are so supportive of other people – now is the time to invest in your own needs.

Some of the same planning suggestions for Ivana may apply to you (see section above). Think about having an account that you can access in an emergency. Many times Laura is so caught up in helping others that she fails to plan for her own crisis. When the spouse comes home and says it is all over, there is frequently no cushion on which to rely. Be prepared, and work on seeing that it never happens!

Solution #3: Make a budget

Write down your personal financial goals, and decide how you will save money to meet those goals. Yes, you can bring your friends on that trip, but make sure that you have a good time, too. Once you have a budget in place, the likelihood of your staying with that budget is pretty high if you don't lose sight of the goal. Fill out the "Realizing your Dream" table below – and remember that these are your dreams.

Realizing your Dream

Your Value/Dream	Financial Goal	Results

Martha

Solution #1: Loosen up

You can't take it with you! Work on a plan to have some fun with your money. What is it that you'd really like to do, but in the past have restrained yourself from doing? Maybe a beach house? A convertible? A vacation to the Caribbean? Come on, you must have some dreams. Start slowly. Spend some money on something less expensive that you would love, like a 10-course dinner at a French restaurant. You probably have worked very hard on saving your money for the future. So what better time than the present to enjoy some of it?

You may need some help with this. Work with a trusted friend on ways that you can loosen up. This friend could probably tell you of ways that you

could have some fun since she knows your likes and dislikes. If this friend is also a Martha, work on ways together to break down some of the structure.

Solution #2: Be flexible with your plans

Martha can get into the rut of "that's the way it has always been done." Because of her tendency to think in the past, she sometimes misses out on new ways of doing things. She has already planned for her retirement, examined her insurance needs, and made her will. Every detail is in place.

Hire a trusted financial account to keep you abreast of options for your finances. Now is the time to look for alternatives, just to see that new laws or benefits have not slipped by you.

Solution #3: Expand your budget

We know you already have a budget in place. But have you budgeted for those fun activities? You know you deserve them. You work extremely hard to get everything done just right. Do you have some 'mad' money laying around for those stress-reducing activities? You also need to find your dream. So we recommend that you fill out the "Realizing your Dream" table and live a little.

Realizing your Dream

Your Value/Dream	Financial Goal	Results

~eight~
Work

Since the 1950's, women have made huge steps in changing the kinds of work they do and making an impact on the workforce.

Work is constantly changing, and women have made some great strides. As women, we are no longer limited to the kind of work we do. Yet the wage gap between male and female managers actually widened in the prosperous years between 1995 and 2000. In the communications industry, for example, the gap between male and female incomes had been 14 cents in 1990 but increased to 27 cents during the late 90's. So, as you can see, we still have work to do to achieve equality.

Even though women make up about one-half of the workforce, only 4% of the top earners at Fortune 500 companies are women. Despite the fact that women are now reaching executive heights, only about 7% of the executives are women. And of those women who do hold executive positions, they are more often in lower level management positions where they have less power.

Currently many women are unhappy with corporate America. Women frequently resign after achieving executive positions, citing an intention to spend more time with their families. This seems to be the socially acceptable reason. Many of us still believe we can have it all – but we've learned that we can rarely have it all at once.

Is it possible to have a rewarding career and a family? Does there always need to be conflict when deciding between one or the other? Many women have quit their jobs when the pressures have become too intense. This may be the result of trying to fit into the "good old boys" network. How long are we going to try to fit into a system that is archaic and obsolete? Could a compromise have been worked out prior to the "all or nothing" decision? New rules may have to be made – new standards set to allow women to experience the opportunities that both may offer.

With the trend towards women leaving big companies quickly, it is estimated that by 2005, there will be about 4.7 million self-employed women in the United States. This projection is up 77% since 1983. For men, the increase is only 6 percent. Women leave because they want to work differently, and because they don't want to have to add changing an old system to their job responsibilities. They want to start from scratch by building something new, different, and totally theirs.

Prior to the 1960's women were generally expected to stay at home, especially if they had children. Many felt unable to make a choice to work outside of the home, because societal pressures were so strong.

Nevertheless, these women kept busy with creative projects, both inside and outside their homes. They weren't about to let society force them into boring routines. These housewives could be called the first free agents. It was rare that any woman sat at home and did nothing. Volunteer programs thrived with the help of very innovative, business-type women. Many women started home businesses in crafts or other clever operations, which helped them look as though they were conforming to societal standards, while giving them an outlet they craved.

Today's women have greater opportunity to choose to stay at home or work outside the home. Some women feel the pressure to work outside the home just to make ends meet. Some have limited choices, especially when they are the sole support for themselves or their family.

But even though the choices may seem limited, the options could be endless if we look at the choices that are available. Some of us allow the "golden handcuffs" of our jobs interfere with choice. Sometimes we think we have to make the all or nothing choice when we could start following our passions on a part-time basis. If you really want to change jobs or be independent, what is keeping you from taking an evening class or working toward that dream job?

Despite our progress, statements such as: "A women's place is in the home" still cause women to feel they are somehow bad or neglecting motherhood responsibilities because they go to work outside the home every day. Why else would they work at home before they go to their job, then work at their job, and then go home and work until well into the evening? The cause is usually guilt feelings from family, friends and society. Many of us don't even recognize what we are actually doing to our bodies. We have to stop sacrificing for the perceived good of everyone else. Will our families and friends be better off if we kill ourselves by sacrificing for them? We need to set priorities about how much work we can do and still stay healthy.

The pendulum swung so fast in moving women from home life to work life that no one set the standards. It just happened. Now we are finally working on how to find balance, fun, and creativity. In the past, most women did not give themselves permission to live their lives. It is still hard for some to break out of old habits.

Having a choice about what we need for ourselves is extremely important. Spend time contemplating what is most important to you. Try for a moment to set aside the cultural, family, and social pressures that are affecting your actions, feelings and behaviors. What is missing for you professionally? What have you dreamed of doing some day?

Many of us have a need to do fulfilling work because of the need to express ourselves beyond our current roles. If we give ourselves time and space, we can begin to remember our dreams of doing something challenging or something that will make a difference. This drive is what causes some of us to reach out into uncharted territories. Being a wife or a mother can be most fulfilling to some, but for others it is not enough. Allow yourself to dream, then start to develop a plan of action toward living that dream. You are never too old to start. What if Grandma Moses had said that she was too old to start painting?

Entrepreneurial ventures are not for everyone, but we are moving toward

an era of the free agent economy. We need to change the way we think about jobs, both within and outside of organizations. As William Bridges, a leading change consultant, advises, "Forget jobs; look for the work that needs doing."

Downsizing is not going away. It's time we begin thinking of ourselves as "Jane Doe, Inc.," regardless of whether we're within or external to an organization. Nowadays no company can be relied upon to take care of us. Times have changed. We have a choice to feel like victims or feel empowered. Our personality and preferred behavioral style will make a difference in how long it takes us to adjust.

Be aware of how you adapt to changes in the work environment. It is easier when we have set ourselves up to make choices. Now is the time to have an alternate plan in place. No job is secure. The sooner that we accept that reality, the more prepared we will be. It doesn't have to be either an organization or a free agent status. It can be a combination of both, if that is your choice. When change does happen, it is much healthier to be able to declare, "I've just been given a chance to do what I've always wanted to do."

Co-author Liz Peterson has worked with many people who have just been fired because of downsizing, rightsizing, mergers and acquisitions. She is amazed at how many people thought their job was secure and believed they wouldn't be affected. The loss of jobs is affecting some of the most competent, intelligent people. It seldom matters who you are or what you do. What's more, it is sometimes impossible to understand the process an organization is using in deciding who to lay off and who to keep. Regardless of whether you're a person who has lost her job or one who has survived the layoff, you are affected and need to work through the loss.

The faster you can get through the anger and resentment at your company for laying you off, the faster you can move on to new opportunities. Have your resume ready at all times and keep your network active. Be ready to send it off to another company or look at other options. Over one-third of the work force is now in the free agent category, some by choice and others by chance.

Women start more businesses that are successful than men! Usually we plan more extensively and think more thoroughly about what we really want to do. Keeping connected and matching our strengths to the ever-changing market are key to success. In general, women understand well the importance of connectedness and are usually more willing to ask for help when it's needed.

Most of us women know that the old command-and-control structures, inspired by the military, are simply not effective anymore. Companies will not keep the energetic, creative people employed in an uninspiring, dull environment. They will not build accountability into systems by controlling the work environment. This is the paradox of giving up control to gain control in the new economy. Women are building new companies where people work differently ... one in which lives are lived honestly. It is a world where people are integrated, not delegated.

Hillary

Solution #1: If you aren't THE BOSS, stop acting as though you are

With your tendency to be dominant, you will probably want others to follow you. This is fine if you are the project manager or THE BOSS. If you are not top dog, the boss may get very tired of your telling others what to do or seeing you go ahead without the input from the team. Teamwork is the most efficient and effective way to get a project completed.

It may be very difficult for you to be on a team. Most companies today are promoting the synergistic benefits of teamwork. Even though you probably espouse the theory that teams are more productive, you don't necessarily like it. Learn where your skills best fit, and communicate clearly where you could most benefit the team. Work on that part of the project. Your team will respect you for staying out of their work, and commend you on the skills you have when leading your phase of the project.

Solution #2: Command & control management does not produce accountability in people

If you are the team leader or THE BOSS, work on letting go of control. If you trust people to complete their work using their own methods, people will be more vested in their jobs and try to give you 110 percent. When you don't trust them and try to control them, you will assume the responsibility for their actions. If you continue to control them, don't be surprised when they sit back and wait for you to tell them what to do. This approach only inspires conformity and lack of creativity.

Control is very difficult to give up. Hire people you trust, and trust them. This is easy to say but not to do. If you are not part of the hiring process, help the hiring staff understand techniques to assure that the person is a good fit for your department.

Work with a coach or mentor who can point out to you when you are taking back control. Picture yourself letting go of control with an outcome that is positive and energizing.

Solution #3: Accept the fact that other people do not accept change as quickly as you do

With your tendency to view your environment as unfavorable, you may be trying to change something that's not really broken. You know you have control over the environment, so think twice before you try to change it. Business books will tell you that most change does not work. That's probably because the people do not feel vested in the change.

If something needs changing, slow down the process. Just because you proclaim that things are to be done a different way today, that won't automatically propel people into implementing the change. People need to feel they are a part of the change in order to own it and make the necessary changes. If all of a sudden they get an edict from above to change, what you will get is resistance.

Solution #4: Others can help you reach the best solution

It probably is very difficult for you to take the time to hear others' suggestions. But doing so could save you time later on. Ivana, Laura and Martha can help you gain a different perspective, by pointing out something you may have overlooked in your quick decision-making process.

Slowing down the decision-making process tends to irritate you. Focus on the positive results you can achieve by taking time to listen. The more you understand the positive qualities of others, the less you have to grit your teeth and try to tolerate them. Patience has never been your strong characteristic. Focus on the strengths of your co-workers. Sometimes it's the people with the slow, methodical thinking process who can be amazingly brilliant with outcomes.

Ivana

Solution #1: If you feel things aren't going well at work, there may be better solutions than rallying the troops or quitting

You tend to see your work environment as favorable. But if things start to become uncomfortable, watch out! You also tend to feel you have control over your environment, so look at the positive options first. You tend to try to change an environment when it does not feel favorable to you.

When you see a problem, bring a solution to your boss or your team and work with others to find the best solution. Sometimes your impulsiveness can get in your way. Your tendency to make hasty decisions can backfire on you – especially when your job is at risk. Remember that life, like grass, is not always greener on the other side of the fence. Every job has its downside. The better you become at resolving issues, the more you will be valued by your boss and your company. Use your energy for positive change.

If you exhaust the best solutions, then it may be time to form some kind of group action, or quit. But try not to use this as your first response. You'll get the reputation of being a troublemaker or a job-hopper.

Solution #2: Find a team member to deal with the details

Since details may take all your energy, ask someone who loves to do detail tasks to help you. When you need to write policies and procedures, find someone who likes to write specific regulatory data. You can do the broad scope work to help them see the bigger picture.

Everyone has strengths and weaknesses. It is because of our strengths that we are weak in other areas. But do keep in mind that an overused strength can become a weakness; you become one-dimensional.

Solution #3: Use your social skills to advance your career

In the corporate arena, this maxim still holds true: it's not so much what you know as who you know. Spend time with people who can advance your career goals. Find a mentor who will help you direct your energy to meet your goals. Watch middle and upper management to determine who has the power to assist you. Very few, if any, persons ever get an executive position without help from some influential person.

Spending time on the phone with your friends, or socializing at the copy machine, may only cause you problems. Try to get some of your social needs met during breaks or at group functions outside of work.

Laura

Solution #1: Tell others about your accomplishments, especially your boss

Start practicing by giving others bits of information about how good you are. Doing this is not bragging. If you don't learn to tell others about what you have done, you may be the first one fired during a re-organization. Management doesn't have time to see all the good things you do.

Of course you find it more comfortable not to talk about yourself. This is where you need to get out of your comfort zone. After all, what's the worst thing that could happen when you tell others about the good things you have accomplished? Start saying things like: "I completed the entire assignment ahead of schedule, and with no errors."

Solution #2: Learn to say NO

The next time someone has another project for you, tell him you would really like to help him, but you have already taken on too many responsibilities. Tell him that you may be able to make some suggestions, but taking on the entire project may jeopardize your job. Be aware that you usually feel bad when you feel someone does not like you. Remind yourself that you can change, calm your fears and know that nobody will ever like you 100% of the time – no matter what you do!

If your boss is the one who has asked you to take on another project, check to make sure you've reminded her of the many projects you are already working on. Don't whine or complain; be assertive and genuine.

Write it down and practice saying it to a friend or to the mirror.

Solution #3: Ask for help

You have a tendency to see your work environment as favorable, even when it isn't. You have learned to tolerate and adapt to many situations! You also see yourself as less powerful than the environment, so you tend not to do much about an intolerable situation. This can keep you from asking for help, while suffering silently. Sit there too long and it will affect your self-confidence.

You don't have to sacrifice all your energy helping others. If you have too much on your plate, ask for help. Most work environments are extremely busy right now. Everyone has more work than she knows how to handle, but you will have more than others. You've always been such a great worker, taking on extra just to help out. What will people think of you if you ask for help?

Start thinking of yourself. This is not selfish! If you start putting in all the hours you need to accomplish your work, you will burn out. When you reach burnout, you will be no good to anyone – including yourself. Here is another place where you can practice asking for help. Start by asking a small favor; then progress up to the bigger favor.

Solution #4: Change does not have to be bad

Get the book **Who Moved My Cheese** and read it. Businesses need to change in order to survive. Pay attention to things that are changing within your environment. Start to make proactive moves that will put you in charge of the change. If your position will be eliminated, where might you fit to continue working for the company? You believe strongly in loyalty to a company. The only problem is that most companies are no longer interested in loyal employees. They want productive employees who produce results.

Start to change the way you think about work. Think about how you can best survive in this type of environment. Continue to assess your skills and how they match with what the company needs. If you need some more special skills for what you want to do, take some extension classes.

Business no longer takes charge of your learning, so you must. Many companies still have benefits that pay for classes. Figure out how you can take advantage of that education benefit. If there is no education benefit, many schools offer classes for a reduced fee. Don't put yourself into the position where you feel the company is responsible for your growth and development. Remember: you are the CEO of Laura, Inc.

Martha

Solution #1: Your work does not have to be perfect to be acceptable

There are certain quality standards that will be important to any company, but sometimes you want your work to be more than perfect. Speed is a much more valued asset than perfection in this economy. Look at Microsoft, which is probably not your favorite company. The customer has become the tester for many of their products that have been sent to market before the defects were removed.

You don't have to compromise quality for speed. You can have both speed and quality. It doesn't have to be all or nothing. And you are probably the best person to find a process that will include both, without compromising the product or service.

Solution #2: Other team members do have skills that are necessary for workflow

Start paying attention to the skills that others add to the team. You need someone who is the idea person, someone who is the follow through person, someone who refines the project, someone who implements the project, and someone who facilitates the process. No one person will do all of these functions well. Determine what you do best, and respect others who add the other functions. While others may not be as conscientious as you are, respect them for the skills they add in bringing efficient results and maximum productivity.

Solution #3: Be prepared for change

You have a tendency to see the work environment as unfavorable. But unlike Hillary, you do not think you have the power to change the environment. In fact, you prefer not to change anything. Now this is a problem in a fast changing, fast paced environment.

Push yourself to get involved with the change initiatives. Volunteer to be on the transition committee. This will prevent you from thinking that you are a victim when the change happens. As with Laura, read the book **Who Moved My Cheese**. Proactive behavior is much more productive than reactive.

Since you probably socialize infrequently with co-workers, you may be the last to know about some obvious changes. Every three months, assess your work situation. Are there small things that have happened that may be a leading indicator for change within the organization? Is your job secure? Are your skills viable in this market? If any of these answers cause you discomfort, determine your action plan and take the necessary steps.

Update your resume, listing your accomplishments and the results to the company. Keep in contact with your networking group. They will be the ones who can probably help you find another position if that need becomes imminent. The more organized you are in this process, the more secure you will feel.

~nine~
Passion, Creativity & Spirituality

We are all looking for something.

Call it peace...truth...meaning...happiness.

For some women, the search for this something gnaws at us like a gnat that continually hovers around our head. For others of us, this search for something enters our consciousness when a circumstance in our lives presents itself – an occasional sadness or frustration, or the continual muddle and ordinary drain of life. Still others, perhaps those of us more deeply in pain, reach a conclusion that this something either does not exist or for some reason will constantly evade us.

Ultimately, that something must be discovered within us. When we take that journey of discovery and become committed to our pilgrimage, we find answers, reach a state of fulfillment, and make sense of our own existence.

Co-author Linda McCabe's mom, whether having a bout of depression or just observing life, would so often ask, "What are we here for; what's it all about?" Of course, no answer satisfied her. She just seemed fascinated with the wondering or pacified by the exercise of just asking. Haven't we all, at one time or another, felt like Alice in Wonderland tumbling into a nonsensical adventure where reality did a disappearing act on us? Or, as in Joseph Heller's **Catch-22**, a protest novel that satirizes the power of modern society to destroy the human spirit, many of us have, at times, felt that squeeze of being in a place where any solution seems inappropriate or out of reach.

The notion that we house the source of our own revelations can be frightening and overwhelming. Akin to this search is the feeling of aloneness.

Mostly we spend our lives in the stuff of everyday life, caring about materialistic needs, the workings of our relationships, how we look, secrets to staying younger, our jobs and careers, the best bargain or the latest fad. The need, however, to go deeper, to find something bigger than ourselves exists in each of us, interrupts our daily lives, and announces itself with regularity.

This search for something, the call to have a purpose, to relate to greater meaning in the universe can be identified as passion, creativity, or spirituality. In this chapter, we will contemplate these concepts, examine our connectivity to them, and consider our choices as they interplay with our lives. We will also explore to some degree the aspect of these words in terms of being a woman.

The differences in meaning of the words passion, creativity, and spirituality can seem blurry. So that we can appreciate the application of the solutions in this chapter, some of Webster's definitions follow:

Passion – the state or capacity of being acted on by external agents or forces; a strong liking or desire for or devotion to some activity, object, or concept.

Creativity – the ability to create. Create – to bring into existence; to produce or bring about by a course of action or behavior; to produce through imaginative skill.

Spirituality – the quality or state of being spiritual; Spiritual – an animating or vital principle held to give life to physical organisms; soul; disposition of mind or outlook especially when vigorous or animated; of or relating to sacred matters.

Hopefully, what may be learned in this chapter will help us capture the essence of these words of Julia Cameron, "Leap and the net will appear."

Hillary

Solution #1: Change your mind

Have you ever done that? Perhaps you were in your car and were driving to the dry cleaners to pick up the items you had cleaned, and then decided to head to the library first instead. Or, you intended to get ready for bed, and instead stayed to watch that late night TV show. Making a decision to do one thing instead of another ... changing your mind. The terms for a platform of thinking can be referred to as a mindset or attitude.

As you have seen, control over events is of the utmost importance to you. However, what is also important to you is creating results. You are so very, very busy working your butt off to produce the results you want in life. If you feel in touch with yourself right now, if you feel that you have attained the happiness that you've expected, if you have an overriding sense of peace – then you can stop reading right now! No need to go any further.

More likely, you are chasing your own tail, running around organizing your life, your job, your children's lives, etc. The things you have been working to control, such as getting the plum assignment, winning the award, having the nicest house, the most expensive clothes, or whatever is on your list, are what have been driving you. Most likely, there is this place inside your head that cries out to you and says, "Do more, get more, you're not there yet." (Wherever there may be.) What is the purpose of trying to get all those things, to get to that job, that relationship, that place of recognition? To make us happy, right?

That brings us back to mindset and attitude. Even though we have heard this before, the concept eludes us: happiness is not a place to get to. It is not something we obtain by accumulating money or objects, or something we can pick up by getting the most degrees, the cleanest house, or the tightest abs. Rather, it is inside us. Inside our hearts and minds.

Change your mind. Override the drive and go directly for the results. You can still do the things you are doing, particularly if you enjoy doing them. However, first start with the realization that circumstances will change, people won't do what you want them to do, and you will not be able to control yourself to happiness, inner peace, or spiritual fulfillment. Looking outside of yourself for happiness will perpetuate the same emptiness, disappointments, and longing.

It is likely that with your behavioral style, you do not find peace and happiness from staring at a beautiful flower, listening to the rainfall, or watching the sunlight play through the trees. Yet, you can decide to make decisions to be happy whether you go the cleaners first or the library. Whether you get the promotion or not, whether you weigh five pounds more today, whether you were invited to that particular party or not, whatever the circumstance. You have that power within yourself regardless of the results. It's a decision. Change your mind.

Solution #2: Use both feet

Imagine trying to stand on just one foot with no other support. After awhile, you'll either tire and give up or fall. Ah, balance! You certainly are the expert at balancing. Balancing your outer life that is. You pretty much have the accumulations of your life in place, and have all the times, places, events and activities in order. Inner balance, however, may be a bit more difficult for you.

So that you as a person – a peaceful, happy person – can exist along with your outer self, feeling comfortable and relaxed while still being productive, you must become familiar with your "shoulds." You know the "shoulds," don't you? They are those harassing instructions in your head that you believe you are supposed to be following. A few examples: "I should call my mother." "I should agree to do that volunteer job." "I should complete that report today."

Creating balance and ridding yourself of the overriding "shoulds" can be accomplished by being in the moment, by being mindful. Not being mindful may be easy for you to understand if you recall chomping down some food and the next minute not remembering you ate it or what it tasted like. While worrying about the next task to follow, you forgot you wrote that check or the amount of the check. You forgot where you put your keys or your glasses when you were rushing to get into the car to get to the next place you were already too late to get to in time. So being mindful means experiencing what you are doing, seeing, or feeling at the moment.

Being mindful also means suspending judgments. It requires not forming opinions about others, the house, the job, the time, or whatever else you are used to thinking all the time. Allow yourself to actually have an experience, i.e., enjoy the smile of a child instead of worrying about her performance at school that day, taste the cookie instead of considering what you have to buy for dinner, hear birds or laughter instead of the deadline at work. Set a goal to become mindful throughout your day as much as possible. You will be amazed at how the inner peace you feel energizes you later for all that you have to do.

Meditation is likely not the appropriate solution for you. Therefore, develop a technique to remind you to be mindful. Choose from one of the possibilities below or create your own to bring about a state of mindfulness and inner balance.

• Write a mantra or prayer or find one in a library book that is short. One you can read every day at a certain time of day.

• Choose a picture or painting that particularly resonates beauty and peace for you (there are sites on the internet that have lovely pictures you can print out and carry with you) and look at it when you rise, after lunch, and after dinner.

• Buy a pin or ring that you particularly enjoy, and throughout the day notice it to bring you back to mindfulness.

• Carry a picture of loved ones and plan (put on your daily schedule) to look at it at certain times throughout the day to recreate a spiritual state.

• Perhaps you drink a cup of coffee, tea or water at various times throughout the day. Make a mental agreement with yourself that every time you feel the liquid passing through your throat, it signals you to return to a mindful state of being.

Solution #3: Bring out the Picasso in you

Along with finding balance and inner peace, we all have a need to express ourselves. If you look at where you live, the people with whom you surround yourself, your furnishings, your work or job, the clothes you wear – all of those are expressions of who you are. Perhaps once you have used a technique from the previous recommendation, you will become aware of the importance and value of mindfulness, and you will be better able to reconstruct the manner and result of your self-expression.

Self-expression displays your creativity. When we create, we express from within the world we see around us, and that can range from that which is directly in front of us to the cosmos. In so doing, we get back in touch with that which is other than ourselves. This in turn allows us to explore, seek to understand and give meaning to that which is the world we live in, and give expression to our experiences.

For our purposes here, creativity for you can be taking on a project, having fuller or greater creativity, or developing creativity that is more reflective of who you feel you really are in your everyday life.

One way to truly avoid creativity in your life is by being constantly busy. How sad, for as noted above, absence of creativity robs a person of being able to truly appreciate and enjoy life to the fullest. In addition to being more mindful, a key for you to becoming more creative is to take action – to do some things which may initially feel uncomfortable, but in the long run generate a more comfortable, peaceful you. Choose from a few suggestions below:

• Carve out time for you to be alone

• Go out to a hobby store. Find and purchase something that you can tolerate that will put you in a different state than the one to which you are normally accustomed. It can be embroidery, woodcraft, painting, decoupage or any craft that enables you to work with your hands and find the artist within you. Just make the time to do it. The result doesn't have to be a masterpiece, and no one but you needs to see it.

• Go to a toy store – browse through it and find something that strikes your fancy. Buy it and play with it a few times a week. This will bring out the long ago tamed child within you and release your inner spirit.

• Visit the forest preserve or someplace peaceful and beautiful. Allow yourself some time to simply see, hear, and feel your surroundings.

• Buy some peaceful music and listen to it with headphones. At the same time, sit with blank sheets of paper and crayons, markers, or colored pens in front of you. Don't try to do anything. Just sit there until something happens (or not).

Ivana

Solution #1: Does it really matter?

You most likely have such a good time socializing, and generally feel so strongly about getting attention from others, that you may have a disconnect between what you do and what really matters to you. Since much of your effort is devoted to people-related activities and concerns, you may feel a lack of motivation, almost an annoying sense that there could be more meaning in life. You may find yourself questioning why you are even going through the motions sometimes. However, an easy way to get back to feeling in touch with yourself and having a deeper feeling of purpose is to discover what is important in your life. Having passion results from finding what really matters.

However, if we are going through life without passion, the realization can come and hit us with a major wallop that can produce a major setback. To discover whether you have passion about something, you may have to spend some time noticing how you feel, as opposed to going through the motion of an activity or being on automatic. You did some of this work back in Chapter One.

To discover how you feel, ask some questions. When you are at work, are you excited about possibilities, do you feel as if what you're doing is fun and fulfilling? When you are in a social situation or in the middle of a conversation with a friend, are you truly engaged? Do you really care about what the other person is saying to you? Something can be mundane, but still really matter. For instance, if a mother drives her children in car pools several times a week, that may not be exciting per se. However, being a conduit for one's children, to bring happiness, activity, enjoyment, or learning experiences to one's children is something most mothers can get very passionate about.

Do an inventory for a couple of weeks. Check out how you are feeling about what you spend your time doing. To determine whether you have passion for it, ask yourself while in the midst of something, "Does this really matter to me?" Doing this will give you some clarity about meaning in your life and help direct you to feeling more connected and content. You can then plan on decreasing activities that leave you with an emptiness or lack of meaning, and begin to get excited about finding ways to spend your time on this earth more passionately.

Solution #2: Getting into your flow

You have within you a natural capacity for expressing who you really are. Finding greater passion will help you explore your deepest feelings. Since seeking approval from others is an important style for you, the real you could be buried beneath your drive to please others. You may also have a tendency, especially when you feel pressured, to become scattered or disorganized in your efforts or activities. To spark that sense of living more fully, to restore balance, to function from your own sense of self, you must take a path toward getting into your flow. A recent example to explain flow is to think of how basketball superstar Michael Jordan was so often described as being "in the zone."

Being in the zone or flow is being in an altered state of consciousness that is both satisfying and forceful or productive. It is a state of creativity. It is a state in which you feel natural and in touch with something greater than yourself. Instead of that sense of disconnect, there is oneness between your mind and your activity. It is a state in which the concept of time disappears and you are in a state of enjoyment. There is no scattered feeling; there is no drive to get something done. Instead, there is an absence of worry or the need to please. Those concerns are replaced with feeling right with what you are doing.

How can you start to reach this flow state? Another way to ask that question is, how can you become inspired? The answer is, turn to the artist in you.

Before we explore ways to reach your artistic self, it is necessary to discuss some areas of caution. First, convince yourself and insist with yourself that you will take the time to rest. Becoming creative cannot happen unless you slow down enough to allow your muse to exist. You will squelch any spark of creativity unless you reduce your pace. The best way for you to do that is to actually schedule the time in your planner.

Next, make an agreement with yourself that you will be totally non-judgmental about the results of your creativity. Within a flow state, judgment simply does not exist. You must decide not to set standards about the process or the results. Just allow the process to be.

Now back to the artist within. Some avenues to explore: poetry, music, journaling, gardening, solitude, hiking, visiting museums, photography, sculpting, painting, cooking…. Think about these for a while. Most likely one of these arts will strike you. If not, visit your library and browse. Have fun.

Solution #3: Spiritual well being and the cycle of life

Our relationship to spirituality is a concept that's individualized to each of us. However, there are some common terms most of us can relate to such as higher self, soul, or a spirit of wisdom. Since you are comfortable being with people, make friends easily, enjoy talking and socializing with others, you can be quite influential. So one way for you to create wellness for your own spirit, one way for you to express your higher self, may be through contribution to others.

You as a woman have a wonderful opportunity to make a difference to others. As women, we have a deep connection to the natural ebb and flow of life. We have a rhythm in our own biological lives. As women we also have a need to nurture, and we can combine this need to nurture with the opportunity to develop our sense of self. We can use these inherent female qualities and continue the basic life cycle by giving to others.

Use your natural empathy by performing acts of kindness for others. Perhaps share your wisdom by mentoring younger women. Find a way to use your connectivity with others through service projects in your community. Look for a cause that touches your heart, and to which you could give your time and talent. Be a good friend by providing support that will help someone through a tough time.

In other words, enrich your own spiritual connectivity and growth through service to others. Strengthen the feminine cycle; we enrich ourselves through doing for others. Giving and doing contributes to the circle of oneness of us all, our connectivity, and our spirituality.

Laura

Solution #1: Travel within

For each of us, there is a center within that, with the right contact, we can find. That center has a wellspring of wisdom. If we think about this, we can probably recall times when we were aware of its existence. It feels like a natural knowing; something just there, reachable without effort, a place where the answer is. We may be more familiar referring to this center of wisdom as soul, spirit, or vital force. Whatever we call this place within us, it is important that we get in touch with this center regularly for us to feel alive and reach some serenity in our lives. In order to make it through our everyday lives or to accomplish our goals, reaching our soul and getting in touch with this center of wisdom is essential.

Most often, you will seek support from others for your spiritual contact, and that is certainly fine. However, looking inward may be more rewarding for those times when you feel you need guidance on your path, or when you feel confused or uncertain, or when you feel unconnected with anything or anyone.

Just as we use certain tools or rituals for taking a trip to a physical destination such as road maps, packing our suitcases, buying tickets, checking the tires on the car, etc., we can make use of these for our journey to our spiritual place.

Try some of these, and plan to do this on a regular basis such as monthly or bimonthly.

• Visit a bookstore or library to find some spiritual books to guide you.

• Purchase meditation tapes.

• Write a prayer or affirmation that is personally yours and use it regularly during your designated times for this activity.

• Go on nature walks.

• Find some music that helps you reach your center.

- Find a picture or sculpture and study it for its meaning and what it means to you.

- Swim, take a bath, or sit next to a pond, since water often aids the contact with our inner selves.

- Work in the garden.

- Use candles or pleasant aromas.

- Make regular visits to a spa

Solution #2: Tap to your beat

Because you most often feel more comfortable being a part of a crowd as opposed to marching to the beat of your own drummer, you may think you are not a creative person. The basic pulse of life, nature itself, must be creative. We are part of nature and life, and therefore, must be creative. Without the experience of creativity, we feel flat, automatic, as if we have truly dried up.

Since you tend to function best with others, there are ways to nurture your creativity without struggling on your own. Here are some ways for you to tap into your own creativity:

- Take a class at an art school.

- Attend a class at a museum; call around and see what you can find.

- Log on to the internet and find a course offered from "The Artist's Way: A Spiritual Path to Higher Creativity," which was inspired by Julia Cameron's well-known book.

- Call places of worship in your community. They often offer classes in creativity.

- Community centers also offer interesting classes to stimulate creativity.

- Use your level of comfort by asking others around you if they know of any creativity classes.

Solution #3: Plug it in and watch the spark

Your behavioral style does not lend itself to a vibrant display of your passion. Your style more often is subdued and quiet. You certainly are not driven to draw attention to yourself with a splashy display of your individual passion for something. This does not mean that you don't feel excitement, or that you don't experience reactions to what you really like or to what really matters to you.

However, one must express oneself in order to feel balanced and to be healthy. It is essential that you find your own way to reflect who you really are. An interesting way to express your passion is to consider the oneness between all things and all beings. All major spiritual disciplines express a doctrine of true connectivity among everything on earth. A successful path for your self-expression would be something that involves your passion for people involvement. You feel most connected amongst others. You feel most whole and alive sharing yourself with others. So, plug it in. Choose activities and even work that connects you with people, and then enjoy your spark, your passion.

Your passion then could be expressed by choosing professions that lend themselves to serving others, such as nursing, ministry, and teaching. A great way to express your passion would be through volunteering. Consider volunteering at your children's school, at nursing homes, homeless shelters, environmental groups, charities, and political campaigns. Think about which of these choices is more appealing to you or, again, use the internet or your library to find other possibilities. Then, make your phone calls or visit websites to sign up. Most importantly, physically get to the place you have chosen and volunteer your services, expertise, and passion to connect with others who can truly use what you have to offer.

Martha

Solution #1: Ah, sweet surrender….

Much of what you do, you do with a strong sense of doing it right. You want order, organization, and accuracy. This same pattern is likely true in your approach to spirituality. Spirit itself is such an elusive concept. And even though theologians have contemplated spirit with trillions of words and centuries of thought, proof in religion and positive judgments about the soul are unlikely. Just as there are countless recipes for savory dishes coming from all over the world and no single one can be unanimously chosen as the only best, the absolute right formula for spirituality is also not very likely. The problem with approaching life from the perspective of "shoulds," judgments, and trying to believe and think the right way, is that the freedom to be yourself, to be in alignment with your own body, mind, and spirit, gets buried in a heavy, prison-like place within you.

Ever notice that after all attempts at analyzing something, considering accuracy and using the ordered way of doing it, mistakes sometimes occur anyway, failure results, or things turn out the opposite of what was expected? Life doesn't offer guarantees. Also, being driven to get the red ribbon for the prettiest, the smartest, or the best project can be exhausting and rarely produces the expected results. After striving for quality and logical approaches, a devastating disease, a weather catastrophe, or a traffic accident can quickly topple the "and they lived happily ever after" ending.

Knowing your values, acting out of what is true for you rather than what is right or wrong, good or bad, logical or not is ultimately what will lead you to a sense of rightness, to your own authenticity and peacefulness. Let go of the constraints of trying to make everything make sense in order to make your world comfortable. At times, surrender to your feelings instead of your judgments, to your heart and not cultural confines, to an intuitive awareness and not fabricated societal confines. Practicing this process of surrender will give you a sweet freedom along with a wonderful right-feeling sense of being in touch with yourself and connected with the universe.

Here are some ideas to help you capture this idea of surrender:

• Purchase and play some board games that require quick and often silly responses, and do not allow for deep consideration and contemplation.

• Go for a splurge shopping spree where the object of your excursion is to pick, perhaps, five items under $20 that are either attractive or appealing for no reason whatsoever except that they seem fun to have.

• Go see a theatre improv production and allow yourself to laugh and see the pleasure in unstructured, unplanned behavior.

• Plan a day, perhaps once a month, where you leave a wide open space of unplanned activity. When the day and time arrive, choose what you feel like doing. Two rules: you cannot do "nothing," and no work of any kind allowed.

• Buy a lottery ticket.

Solution #2: Step out of your comfort zone

Because you are so much more at home with a logical approach to most of life, operating from loose, unstructured, free expression may feel somewhat uncomfortable. If you want to be more creative, it will be necessary to step outside of your norm where you feel most protected and leap a bit. Take the plunge into that cold pool of life.

You might ask: "Why would I want to do that?" Because creativity is an expression of our souls. Creativity just is, within us all. From a mother giving birth, to lovers embracing, scientists finding a new cure, a teacher finding a new path to help a student, to someone who having lost a loved one starts a new charity to honor that loved one – these are all expressions of our creativity. It is expressions of creativity that help us on our path to growth and purpose.

Also, if you can love yourself, you can trust yourself – and then you can begin to search for your own creativity, venture beyond your more practiced, organized self, and break through your shell, your comfort zone of protection. This may for a while feel in opposition to your basic nature, even feel silly, and truly feel as if you are stepping out into the unknown. However, after awhile, you'll probably be very surprised at how free you will feel, how the inner you will be revealed, and how you will be able to view the world from new perspectives.

As to how to begin, be honest with yourself. Make a decision not to judge. This is for you and you alone, and in this one case, whatever feels right and natural to you is good. Warning: Allow yourself the experience of falling on your face, to fail, at first. That's part of this process. Make a decision that you will be safe, have fun, and enjoy this part of life beyond your normal boundaries.

Solution #3: Feel the zest!

Of course, you already have felt passionate about many people and things. However, it is possible you have been restrained a little given your inclination toward perfectionism. Remember, passion is what matters most to you. Try some of these exercises to get in the mood to experience passion about something important to you:

• Remember a time in your life when you felt truly excited – just about jumping out of your skin with glee. Recall how it felt. Then try to hold on to that zestful feeling until it's familiar enough that you can recreate it whenever you want it.

• Remember a time when you were basking in the glow of accomplishment. Recall that moment when you knew you did something really terrific and received recognition for it. Again, feel that feeling as you remember, and become familiar enough with it to bring it back in another circumstance.

• Think back to some time when you either had a good, guffawing belly laugh or were acting truly silly. Get in touch with that experience and snap a mental picture, so you can call upon that sense of abandon and that depth of joy to recreate that passion for something else when you want it.

• Truth time…when you are almost falling asleep, when you are in that very secret space, when you are forming dreams, but not yet asleep – what do you secretly dream? What is it that you would love to come true? Those are the dreams you can get truly passionate about. Then you can use your creativity to turn those dreams into reality.

Do you have any heroes or heroines? Does some celebrity, character in a book, or actual historical person come to mind who you truly admire? Or, perhaps a parent or a teacher from your past has earned your admiration. See if there is a pattern or a quality that emerges. Then, build on that revelation to develop a passion. For instance, Eleanor Roosevelt had so much compassion for the poor or downtrodden. The thought process here could be, "I feel much the same. What can I do to help those in need?" As another example, I recall my aunt Lyl steadfastly watching political TV coverage for hours on end. The thinking process here might be, "I enjoy that as well. Perhaps I will seek out how to express my passion for particular political candidates or volunteer at political functions."

• Go to some quiet physical spot – a lake, a forest preserve, some beautiful, quiet place. Just breathe at first and take in the peacefulness. Then ask yourself these questions:

–How will my life look in 5 years?

–What do I want my life to look like in 5 or 10 years?

–As I look back on my life, what have I truly, deeply cared about?

–At the end of my life, what will I think truly mattered most to me?

You will get some answers that reveal your inner passions and point you in the direction of what you can get really excited about.

Note Pad

Use these pages to jot down ideas, to make and keep plans, to write scripts, to keep time schedules, or to keep lists, records and any thoughts you would like to remember.

Notes

Notes

Notes

Notes

Recommended Reading

Bolton, Michele Kremen, **The Third Shift: Managing Hard Choices in Our Careers, Homes, and Lives as Women**. Jossey-Bass Books, 2000.

Borysenko, Joan, **A Woman's Book of Life: The Biology, Psychology and Spirituality of the Feminine Life Cycle**. Riverhead Books, 1996.

Buckingham, Marcus and Coffman, Curt, First, **Break All The Rules: What The World's Greatest Managers Do Differently**. Simon & Schuster, 1999.

Daniels, Joni, **Power Tools For Women: Plugging into the Essential Skills for Work and Life**. Crown Publishers, 2002.

DeAngelis, Barbara, **Secrets About Life Every Woman Should Know: Ten Principles for Total Emotional & Spiritual Fulfillment**. Hyperion, 1999.

Fezler, William, **The Good Girl Syndrome: How Women Are Programmed to Fail in a Man's World & How to Stop It**. MacMillan Publishing Co., 1985.

Johnson, M.D., Spencer, **Who Moved My Cheese?** New York. G.P. Putnam's Sons, 2002.

Marotta, Priscilla V., Ph.D., **Power and Wisdom: The New Path for Women**. Phelps & Associates, 1999.

McGraw, Phillip C., **The Relationship Rescue**, Hyperion, 2000.

Mosbacher, Georgette, **Feminine Force: Release the Power to Create The Life You Deserve**. Simon & Schuster, 1993.

Richardson, Cheryl, **Stand Up For Your Life**. The Free Press, 2002.

Ritchey, Tom, **I'm Stuck, You're Stuck. San Francisco**. Berrett-Koehler Publishers, 2002.

Sanford, Linda Tschirhart and Donovan, Mary Ellen, **Women & Self-Esteem: Understanding and Improving The Way We Thank and Feel About Ourselves**. Penguin Group, 1978.

Shaevitz, Marjorie Hansen, **The Confident Woman: Learn The Rules of The Game**. Harmony Books, 1999.

Tieger, Paul D. and Barbara Barron-Tieger, **Do What You Are**. Boston, New York, Toronto, London: Little, Brown and Company, 1995.

ISBN 141202174-X